COUNSELLING IN THE VOLUNTARY SECTOR

· COUNSELLING IN CONTEXT ·

Series editors
Moira Walker and Michael Jacobs
University of Leicester

Counselling takes place in many different contexts: in voluntary and statutory agencies; in individual private practice or in a consortium; at work, in medical settings, in churches and in different areas of education. While there may be much in common in basic counselling methods (despite theoretical differences), each setting gives rise to particular areas of concern, and often requires specialist knowledge, both of the problems likely to be brought, but also of the context in which the client is being seen. Even common counselling issues vary slightly from situation to situation in the way they are applied and understood.

This series examines eleven such areas, and applies a similar scheme to each, first looking at the history of the development of counselling in that particular context; then at the context itself, and how the counsellor fits into it. Central to each volume are chapters on common issues related to the specific setting and questions that may be peculiar to it but could be of interest and value to counsellors working elsewhere. Each book will provide useful information for anyone considering counselling, or the provision of counselling in a particular context. Relationships with others who work in the same setting whether as counsellors, managers or administrators are also examined; and each book concludes with the author's own critique of counselling as it is currently practised in that context.

Current and forthcoming titles

Elsa Bell: *Counselling in Further and Higher Education*
Judith Brearley: *Counselling and Social Work*
Dilys Davies: *Counselling in Psychological Services*
Pat East: *Counselling in Medical Settings*
David Lyall: *Counselling in the Pastoral and Spiritual Context*
Michael Megranahan: *Counselling at Work*
Janet Perry: *Counselling for Women*
Gabrielle Syme: *Counselling in Independent Practice*
Nicholas Tyndall: *Counselling in the Voluntary Sector*
Brian Williams: *Counselling in the Penal System*

COUNSELLING IN THE VOLUNTARY SECTOR

Nicholas Tyndall

OPEN UNIVERSITY PRESS
Buckingham · Philadelphia

Open University Press
Celtic Court
22 Ballmoor
Buckingham
MK18 1XW

and

1900 Frost Road, Suite 101
Bristol, PA 19007, USA

First Published 1993

A catalogue record of this book is available from the British Library

ISBN 0 335 19027 8 (pb)

Library of Congress Cataloging-in-Publication Data
Tyndall, Nicholas, 1928–
Counselling in the voluntary sector / Nicholas Tyndall.
p.   cm. — (Counselling in context)
Includes bibliographical references and index.
ISBN 0-335-19027-8 (pb)
1. Counseling.   2. Volunteer workers in social service.
I. Title.   II. Series.
BF637.C6T59   1993
361.3′23—dc20
93-18724   CIP

Typeset by Graphicraft Typesetters Ltd, Hong Kong
Printed in Great Britain by St Edmundsbury Press Ltd,
Bury St Edmunds, Suffolk

Contents

Series editors' preface   vi
Preface   viii

1 · THE DEVELOPMENT OF COUNSELLING IN THE
    VOLUNTARY SECTOR   1

2 · VOLUNTARY AGENCIES   20

3 · THE PRACTICE OF COUNSELLING IN THE
    VOLUNTARY SECTOR   43

4 · SPECIFIC ISSUES IN COUNSELLING IN THE
    VOLUNTARY SECTOR   68

5 · PROFESSIONAL RELATIONSHIPS IN COUNSELLING
    IN THE VOLUNTARY SECTOR   92

6 · A CRITIQUE OF COUNSELLING IN THE
    VOLUNTARY SECTOR   111

Appendix: addresses of voluntary counselling organizations   135
References   139
Index   144

Series editors' preface

Counselling owes much to the volunteer. Perhaps what distinguishes the history of counselling in Britain from that of psychotherapy is that counselling took root initially in a small number of voluntary organizations, and that it is from there that counselling has grown out into many other settings – which later volumes in this series will examine. There must be a large number of counsellors whose first client was seen when they started as a volunteer counsellor or helper in one of the now numerous agencies that provide counselling or that draw considerably in their service provision upon the application of counselling skills. Counsellors who have later taken up salaried posts or entered private practice often 'cut their teeth' in counselling services where the high standards of practice and supervision formed them and prepared them, in a way which no courses alone could, for what appears the more professional and glamorous end of counselling. In fact distinctions between amateur and professional are hard to make in this area, and largely inappropriate. The majority of counselling agencies provide as professional a service as statutory agencies, and are sometimes much better supervised.

We both know well the efficacy of the voluntary counselling service, since we have been intimately involved with such an agency, where counsellors and supervisors, receptionists and consultants all give their time, for no financial reward (not even expenses), and where the few salaried staff give more than they are ever financially compensated for. Nick Tyndall knows such services from a much wider perspective than we do, having played a leading role both in Relate (or Marriage Guidance as it was then) and in Cruse. He is admirably placed to identify the issues that are involved, and to provide a book which supports both existing agencies, and provides much distilled wisdom for those contemplating setting up such counselling services.

Politicians are good at praising the work of voluntary organizations and those who work for them. Many of us know that the work that these counsellors undertake, the level of disturbance which is brought to them, and the good that they do, far exceeds anything that either politicians or county hall administrators recognize. Volunteer counsellors are as much in the front line as any medical practice or social service. The buck frequently has to stop with them because there is nowhere else for desperate people to go, to be seen regularly, and with whole-hearted commitment, at little financial cost. We hope that this book will provide evidence enough to encourage those who make political decisions and who hold purse strings to put their money where their mouth is, so that they make proper provision for those who, remarkably, seldom appear demoralized by the sheer enormity of the demands upon them. We hope too that it will provide encouragement to the thousands of people who have no wish to climb on the professional bandwagon, but who value the counselling relationships which they enter as a proven way of offering care and possibilities of change to other people.

Moira Walker
Michael Jacobs

Preface

My involvement with counselling in the voluntary sector has spanned thirty years. It began in the 1960s when I was at the Prison Service Staff College. We were training staff to have greater understanding in their relationships with prisoners and their families. We encouraged them to be kindly and compassionate, but we had no knowledge of how to train them in personal skills. We searched for ways of helping them to carry out the official objective of 'turning people out of prison better than when they came in'.

I applied to the National Marriage Guidance Council for training, and became a marriage counsellor. The counselling training threw new light on our understanding of the personal and family problems of offenders, and opened up for us avenues of more effective support for prison staff. Subsequently I became director of what is now called Relate; and then training officer for Cruse, where for five years I trained bereavement counsellors.

All three areas of my career have been with people coping with loss – loss of freedom and self-image; loss of happiness and fulfilment in intimate relationships; loss through death – and with training people to give them help and support.

There is much in counselling which is common to these three settings. But there are differences of focus, of emphasis and of setting. This book aims to examine these similarities and differences throughout counselling in the voluntary sector. What is the common core of this art form which has such varied manifestations?

I remember hearing counselling compared to the colour 'yellow'. 'We all know what yellow is,' said the speaker, 'but we can only describe it when linked with a noun – yellow books, yellow flowers, etc.' Likewise, counselling is an activity which has to be described as linked to a life event or a specific setting – redundancy counselling, AIDS counselling or counselling in the workplace. This book explores what makes up this 'yellowness' in the many settings in which counselling is given by volunteers.

The task has not been easy because the settings, and the aspirations of the agencies, vary so greatly. I have found myself continually on a tightrope. On the one side are those travelling hopefully with goodwill, enthusiasm and spontaneity; on the other, those who have become quasi-professional. I do not judge between them, because there is need for them all.

This tightrope reflects the dilemmas in the counselling world – the struggle to improve standards, but in the process trying not to become too elitist; the readiness to encourage new initiatives, but the fear that that enthusiasm may be misplaced; the wish to extend the range of counsellor recruits, but the anxiety that the quality of counselling may then suffer. Each time I come down on one side of the tightrope, I fear I may cause dismay among those on the other side. But I have come to realize that this tension is not only between counselling organizations, it is in each one of us – certainly in me.

What is clear is that there is no going back to the innocence of the Garden of Eden. We now have knowledge and experience. This is being passed on in many voluntary agencies and educational establishments to volunteers of all ages who are becoming the new generation of 'amateurs working to professional standards'.

What is it like to be a voluntary counsellor? What do counsellors actually do? Who are the clients? Does counselling help them? How do agencies organize their counselling? Who carries responsibility for the counselling? In exploring these questions, I draw largely on my experience in marriage and bereavement counselling. However my work in voluntary organizations has brought me into close touch with other agencies in church, health and family settings in Britain and abroad. Chairing an international commission on marriage counselling for many years, and six months on sabbatical leave among family agencies in India, convinced me that there is indeed a common core in counselling and that it has an international dimension.

I am deeply indebted to my tutors and colleagues who have imparted their wisdom to me over the years. There are far too many to name. I am grateful to generations of trainees whose keenness and enthusiasm have often buoyed me up when I was discouraged. And I warmly thank my clients who have allowed me into the intimacy of their lives and who have taught me so much.

They will not recognize themselves in the pen portraits in this book, for these are an amalgam of many different people. My thanks also to the many workers who have taken time to give me the feel of their corner of the voluntary sector. And, finally, thanks to my family who have borne with me in this labour of love; especially to Daniel who has taught me to use an Amstrad, and to my wife Elizabeth for her constant encouragement, advice and patience.

· ONE ·

The development of counselling in the voluntary sector

CRIES FOR HELP

A teenager sits morosely in a temporary hostel warming himself on a cup of tea. He looks suspiciously at the girl, not much older than himself, who has asked him if she can do anything to help him. They begin to talk about why he left home, what his hopes were in coming to London and why he does not want to go back home in spite of his hopes being shattered.

A middle-aged couple perch uncomfortably at opposite ends of their sitting-room and wonder what to say to the visitor who has called from a group they had never heard of, Compassionate Friends. The visitor says she had a son who was killed in an accident on holiday and she knows it helped her to be able to talk about it. Would they like to tell her about how their only daughter had just met her death?

A woman rings a cancer care helpline. She has heard her diagnosis but cannot really believe it. She is still in shock. How can she tell her three children, all living at home and dependent on her? Should she contact her husband who left home a year ago? What will happen to her mother who is becoming senile? Above all, how will she face the few remaining months?

A young woman thinks of writing to an address she saw in a women's magazine. She is fearful to seek out help lest her husband finds out. He gets so angry and demands sex and hits her. Her parents arranged the marriage and she cannot turn to them. She dare not tell anyone else in her community, and she has no friends outside the community to confide in. She wonders what she can do.

A 40-year-old single man is managing in a wheelchair since his motorcycle crash, but he is partially paralysed and is unlikely to work again. He gets depressed about the future. The hospital after-care was excellent at first but now the nurse says he needs more sustained contact to help him to readjust to his new circumstances. The nurse suggests a counsellor might help him to come to terms with the present and to plan for the future.

Two grandparents have consulted a solicitor about their rights to see their grandson who is now in the custody of his mother. She refuses to let the child go to the homes of his father or grandparents. The solicitor explains that the law can be used to enable access to the boy, but first it might be best to try to work out why there was this breakdown in relationships with the daughter-in-law and to see if they can be mended. He wonders if they might talk it over first with a conciliator or counsellor.

All these people might have the chance of seeing a counsellor, and many of the counsellors will be attached to voluntary organizations. The types of assistance on offer are growing year by year. This sometimes makes it difficult to identify the precise nature of all these agencies and to know what sort of help they provide.

People who have not experienced counselling may find it hard to understand how 'just talking' can help. It may well feel like a leap into the unknown. As a colleague once remarked: 'Half the folk out there think their problems aren't serious enough to go for help. The other half think their problems are so overwhelming that nothing can be done to solve them anyway!'

What, then, is this help that is known generically as 'counselling'? This book looks at the counselling services provided by voluntary groups and at how counselling is organized and managed in the voluntary sector. The range of these services is enormous; the diversity so wide that it is impossible to do justice to the richness of this rapidly growing sphere of activity which is based on the commitment and expertise of the thousands of volunteers who form the workforce of the counselling services in the voluntary sector.

THE VOLUNTARY SECTOR

Great Britain can to-day show a system of combined statutory and voluntary services which has grown up in the last forty years, quite peculiar to itself. In no other country in the world can anything on similar lines be found.

(Morris 1955: 175)

This assessment of the voluntary sector made by Elizabeth Mac-adam in 1934 is still valid today. Her praise for the strength of voluntary organizations is fully justified. Her claim for the unique-ness of the scope and high standards of commitment in the volun-tary sector still holds good. Indeed the sophisticated use of volunteers will be one of the main themes of this book, and is a unique de-velopment that still causes wonder and envy in other Europeans and Americans. Alas, her picture of partnership between volun-tary and statutory services has become over-optimistic in the recent past. And her implication that the voluntary services are themselves a coherent entity is wide of the mark. The volun-tary sector is dynamic, innovative and ever changing. But it is a jungle.

The genesis of the voluntary sector lies in the mid-nineteenth century, and was connected with prominent citizens such as Lord Shaftesbury and Dr Barnado. The organizations they founded, which still bear their names, and the pioneer Charity Organisation Society (now the Family Welfare Association) aimed at the relief of poverty and provision of education. These remain the basic criteria which the Charity Commissioners use in determining whether to grant charitable status to new bodies today. However the definition of poverty has been extended to include poverty of lifestyle, and many counselling agencies have become charities on grounds that they relieve the stress and unhappiness associated with poverty of mind, body or soul.

The voluntary sector is now a multifarious collection of organ-izations. It still contains welfare bodies and educational organ-izations, but there are now also religious bodies of all faiths, art and drama associations, an increasing number of groups concerned with minority rights, women's issues and ethnic problems, as well as environmental and recreational bodies. When Elizabeth Macadam wrote, there were 35 voluntary organizations listed in the directory published by the umbrella body, then called the National Council of Social Service (now the National Council for Voluntary Organisations). By 1951 there were 311 entries in it (Morris 1955: 189). The 1992 *Voluntary Agencies Directory* contained nearly 2000.

When the Wolfenden Committee on the Future of Voluntary Organizations (Wolfenden 1978) surveyed the field it identified several categories which included:

(i)   Mutual aid organizations, where everyone is unpaid, such as Alcoholics Anonymous;

(ii)   volunteer organizations, which provide services with vol-
       unteer helpers, such as the Samaritans;
(iii) voluntary organizations, which have paid and voluntary
       workers, such as the Spastics Society;
(iv)   private non-profit-making organizations, which employ
       professional staff backed by voluntary helpers, such as
       Barnados.

(Poulton 1988: 7)

Counselling is offered by agencies in each of these categories. In
total, 125 of those listed in the 1982 *Voluntary Agencies Directory*
specifically stated that they provide a counselling service. These
range from large bodies in which counselling is available via a
network of branches nationally, such as Cruse Bereavement Care;
through those with several sources of help such as Turning Point,
which has 30 projects in various parts of Britain for people with
drug- and alcohol-related problems; to places which provide a small
personal service such as the Grail, the Roman Catholic retreat house
in Pinner.

Some of these agencies offer personal counselling in an office,
some through visits to clients' homes, some by telephone or correspondence. Some use full-time staff as counsellors, some employ
sessionally paid counsellors; but most began by using, and many
still rely exclusively upon, volunteers who undergo in-house
selection, training and supervision within the agency.

The scene is very diffuse. Practice, aims and standards vary greatly.
But what the agencies have in common is reaching out to make a
warm human response to persons in need. As the first chairman of
the pioneering Marriage Guidance Council said, the early counsellors
were spurred on by a sense of compulsion, not by a clear idea of
how they were to achieve their aims but 'as nobody else was trying,
we must needs try' (Holt 1971).

Gradually counselling has acquired the discipline of a profession,
in the sense of an activity which has an accepted code of practice
and ethics and whose practitioners, whether paid or not, submit
their work to the scrutiny and assessment of their peers. The last
decade has seen attempts to agree a system of accreditation for
counsellors. The story of counselling has become one in which the
medium has become the message.

But for many in the voluntary sector the pressure remains on
today's helpers, as on the first pioneers, to make a spontaneous
human response to the person in distress who telephones or walks
into the office. They echo the words of the twelfth-century Abbot

of Rievaulx cited in *Marriage Matters* (Home Office and DHSS 1979: 6):

> So teach me, gracious Lord, to admonish the unruly, to strengthen the faint-hearted, to support the weak; and to adapt myself to each one according to his nature, his way of life, disposition, capacity or simpleness, and according to place or time, as would seem to thee good . . .

Commenting on this prayer, *Marriage Matters* continued:

> For the modern counsellor, as for the mediaeval pastor, the critical point lies in the phrase 'to adapt myself to each one'. Wise counsellors know how wide is the spectrum of possible relationships, and how dangerous it is to invest any method with some ideological or absolute authority which does not belong to it. The test is practically how people are helped best.

In this book I explore how people are currently 'helped best' in the voluntary counselling agencies. I look in detail at some of the organizations, but aim to draw out what might be a common core of practice and organizational structure. I write also to be of use for administrators and committee members, in the hope of encouraging the all too rare sharing of experience and co-operation between agencies.

For innovators who are contemplating introducing counsellors to tackle some new social need, I highlight the strengths and limitations of a counselling service. This may ease the task for them and spare them some of the labour of reinventing the wheel. For trainers, counsellors and would-be counsellors, I examine the satisfactions and demands across the sector. For potential clients, referrers and other users of the services, I try to dispel some of the mysterious aura which tends to surround counselling, so that they may make more informed decisions about whether, when and where to go for help. And I hope it may also assist those who provide funds in making appropriate decisions about how to allocate their donations and sponsorship.

In varying guises counselling is now practised in a wide range of areas in the voluntary sector. Some of these are dealt with in greater detail in other volumes in this series – the churches, women's groups, and young people's agencies. Although this volume touches on those specific interests, I concentrate here on other settings. These include disability groups, ethnic minorities, gay groups, sex and marriage, divorce, conciliation and bereavement.

HISTORICAL DEVELOPMENTS

Writing in Ohio in 1942 about interviews for psychological treatment, Rogers (1942: 3) noted 'they are most frequently termed
counseling, a word in increasingly common use'. Fifty years later
the same can be asserted about Britain. Now with anglicized spell-
ing, counselling has grown rapidly in Britain in recent years, both
as a *modus operandi* of the traditional helping professions and as an
activity in its own right.

'Counselling is a process as old as the hills', wrote Venables (1971:
1), 'and people in crises have always sought out those with a reputation for wisdom to help them solve their problems'. But, she went
on to argue, our increasing ability to solve our material problems by
scientific and technological means has turned our attention to human
relationships, 'which have the power to frustrate the investigations
of the social scientist and give lie to his findings'.

It was in fact in voluntary organizations that counselling as a
defined activity first emerged in Britain. In 1948 David Mace, general
secretary of the National Marriage Guidance Council, published a
book entitled *Marriage Counselling: The First Full Account of the Remedial
Work of the MGC*. The Council had been formed ten years earlier for
the purpose of 'Safeguarding the family unit as the basis of our
community life' (Lewis *et al.* 1992: 272). It initially concentrated on
arranging lectures on pre-marriage education, but soon Mace was
advocating 'a movement parallel to that which has established the
Child Guidance Clinics' in which doctors, clergy and others would
be available for consultations about marriage problems (Lewis *et al.*
1992: 60).

By 1946 the NMGC had already established a scheme for selecting
lay counsellors, based on techniques used by War Office Selection
Boards. A training programme spread over a year, compulsory for
all counsellors, was in place, with an assessment at the end. With a
flash of inspiration which has never been regretted, these pioneers
instituted a stringent selection process right at the beginning, long
before they really knew what they were selecting for. They were
insistent on keeping out busybodies and people who liked exerting
influence. They believed passionately that counsellors are born, not
made; that training can build on natural talent but cannot create a
sensitive listener from unsatisfactory material, any more than singing
lessons can make a musician out of a tone-deaf person.

At the outset one-off interviews were offered with the aim of
discovering clients' main source of difficulty and referring them to
a relevant specialist, such as a psychiatrist, general practitioner,

solicitor, minister of religion or family planning adviser. Most of these early interviews were closed to the satisfaction of the counsellor when a referral was made. Counsellors saw themselves as first-aid workers backed by a team of specialist consultants (Wallis and Booker 1958).

Slowly, however, counsellors themselves became the primary means of help, and became more reluctant to pass clients on to consultants. Eventually the flow reversed, as medical practitioners recognized that many of their patients needed more time and focused attention than they could give themselves and referred them to counsellors to talk over their problems at greater length. Counsellors now saw their clients at regular intervals over a period of time. The emphasis in training came to be on forming and maintaining a counselling relationship for weeks, or even sometimes months.

Similar developments were happening in other voluntary organizations in the period following the Second World War, stemming from the unprecedented amount of marital and family disharmony evident at the end of the war. The Catholic Marriage Advisory Council split off from NMGC in 1946 to provide help with marital issues within the context of Catholic teaching about divorce and contraception. The Family Welfare Association set up a Marriage Welfare sub-committee which subsequently became independent as the Family Discussion Bureau and later became the Tavistock Institute of Marital Studies. Citizens' Advice Bureaux began training some of their workers to deal with marital problems, and the Family Planning Association and the Soldiers', Sailors' and Airmen's Families Association also applied for government funding for such work (Lewis *et al.* 1992: 71). By the 1950s the activity recognizable as marriage counselling was well established, albeit known, as it still is, by various names – marriage guidance, counselling, conciliation, reconciliation or mediation.

In other settings similar work was being developed under different names. As already mentioned, MGC drew much of its inspiration from Child Guidance Clinics, and there the term in most frequent use was 'social casework'. One of the key textbooks in that field was published in Chicago in 1957, 15 years after Rogers first wrote, yet it makes no mention of counselling. But its description of social casework, with its emphasis on the relationship between caseworker and client aiming at developing the latter's effectiveness in coping with his problem, is synonymous with any description of counselling (Perlman 1957: 5).

By contrast the Samaritans, established in London in 1953 as the first telephone helpline, adopted the term 'befriender' for their helpers. Yet, as with counselling, their activity is described as treating callers with 'unconditional uncritical acceptance and respect' and is defined 'as a therapeutic not a social relationship' (Keir 1986: 158). The Samaritans' growth was impressive. Within ten years there were 41 branches. Ten years later there were 160 and by the early 1990s there were 185, attending to nearly half a million new callers every year. Yet, for fear of sounding too professional, the Samaritans are still wary of labelling their well-established listening help as counselling.

A CENTRAL ASSOCIATION

Counselling was a word used in an increasing number of settings in the 1960s, so much so that, in a major step that turned out to have considerable significance, the Standing Conference for the Advancement of Counselling (SCAC) was set up in 1970 by the National Council of Social Service (NCSS). Against a background of some scepticism, it was intended as a forum for practitioners to meet to exchange information and good practice. The word 'advancement' appeared in its title advisedly. But the underlying concern was that counselling was proliferating and seemed to be being offered in some situations without any safeguards or constraints.

Sir George Haynes, the retired director of NCSS, took a leading role in drawing into membership voluntary bodies such as the Spastics Society, the Pregnancy Advisory Service, the Albany Trust, the Westminster Pastoral Foundation and the Salvation Army. He was insistent that the new body would not be viable without the active participation of NMGC, which at that time was acknowledged as the most developed nationwide counselling agency. I was then its chief officer and I agreed to become vice-chairman of SCAC. Likewise, it was thought to be important to have backing from within the medical profession and a psychiatrist, Nicolas Malleson, became the first chairman.

SCAC captured the interest of the main counselling bodies. Some were already in loose professional groupings, and these came into SCAC as divisions, such as the Association of Student Counsellors, the Association of Pastoral Care and Counselling, and Counselling in Education. Other divisions gradually formed – Counselling in Medical Settings, Counselling at Work, and an omnibus group for many of the voluntary organizations not in other groups – the Personal Sexual Marriage and Family division. Harmony was not always possible. As is recounted in more detail in a companion book in this series, the youth counselling division, which joined as the National Association of Young People's Counselling and Advisory Services, eventually left to form its own independent body in 1975.

SCAC provided an information service and created a meeting place through conferences. It achieved the crucially important aim of nurturing counselling as an inter-disciplinary activity across the divides of the paid and the volunteer, the full-time and the part-time, and those for whom counselling was a main task and those who used counselling as an adjunct to some other specialism or profession.

The British Association for Counselling (BAC) grew out of SCAC in 1977. The immediate reason for this transformation was financial. The small priming grant from the Home Office was proving inadequate for SCAC's needs and was likely to dry up completely. It seemed that future funding could only be assured by turning to those who had a vested interest in the development of counselling. The new association therefore sought to rely on fees from its member bodies and from the mushrooming number of practitioners who were joining as individual members. More significantly, however, the change of name and function would never have survived without the demonstrable increase in confidence within the counselling ranks and a common wish to set up a body which would concern itself with standards of service. Counselling was clearly here to stay.

BAC has continued to act as a support to individual counsellors and to counselling bodies in the voluntary sector. In 1992 there were nearly 7500 individuals and over 450 organizations in membership, the latter including local counselling groups, charitable and educational bodies, as well as national organizations. Although much of BAC's energy has gone into the perplexing task of setting up an accreditation system, other issues of immediate relevance to the voluntary sector have been regularly addressed, such as race and cultural education, peace and justice, and disability.

The Association of Pastoral Care and Counselling exemplifies the continual attempt to form a bridge between voluntary and professional counselling. Its membership consists of ordained and paid non-ordained; lay people and those in religious orders; workers in parishes and other formal church settings; chaplains in hospitals, prisons or the armed services; and voluntary counsellors with a religious commitment who feel called to work in secular settings.

BAC's largest division, with around 900 members in 1992, is the one which incorporates most of the counsellors from the voluntary sector. Following the trend, it has dropped 'marriage' from its title and become the Personal Sexual Relationships and Families (PSRF) division.

Inevitably BAC has come primarily to represent the interests of those of its members who are keen on the development of counselling as a career, i.e. those who are paid as counsellors in industry, in universities, in the health service and the like. The beginning of this sort of professional counselling was in schools and emerged through diploma courses specifically for experienced teachers. These began at the universities of Keele, Reading and Aston at the end of the 1960s. Today there are many shorter courses run by institutions of higher education, open to students of all ages and from all backgrounds. Many of these students gain practical experience during their courses by working in a voluntary organization. Some subsequently become counsellors in the voluntary sector. For instance, the Adult Education Department of the University of Leicester has over 500 people attending counselling courses at any one time. Similar demand is experienced at Birmingham and other universities.

DEFINING COUNSELLING

One of the paradoxes of counselling is that, on the one hand, volumes have been written about it, yet, on the other, it draws upon everyday experience in a way which seems so simple and ordinary. The counselling experience may seem like the formal equivalent of neighbours sitting over a cup of tea or a pint of beer and letting off steam about the youngster's tantrums, rows with their partners or worries about the hire purchase. There is nothing special about all these situations. How is it then that counselling has become such a major industry? Why are there so many agencies, so many committees, so much concern about funding?

The answer is that it is not the counselling itself that is complicated. To be sure, there are techniques to acquire which can assist, and there are relevant practical matters to learn. But the process itself, of giving time and attention, of listening to and sharing a problem, perhaps of helping to unravel it and maybe make a decision about it, is a normal caring human response. It requires time, patience and confidence on behalf of the counsellor, but that is not complicated. It is, however, an invitation to step into the unknown, and this can generate anxiety for both counsellor and client. The client weighs up the counsellor, wondering if she can be of help, testing out if he can trust her, perhaps fearing that he may be facing yet another let-down. The counsellor assesses the client in her own mind, listening to his problem, which may start simply but become more complex as it unravels. She probably catches something of the client's feelings of being overwhelmed, so she questions her own ability to be of use. Both wonder how far their relationship can become a safe one for the giving of confidences and the exploring of feelings. Both struggle in their own minds with their expectations and hopes of what can be achieved. And because the counsellor has nothing tangible to give, no prescription pad to hand, no money to lend, only her own personal talents to offer, she can feel very vulnerable.

What is complicated is what flows from making a formal offer to be of assistance, what is entailed in the offer and the consequences that follow in its train. Later chapters examine the responsibility involved in offering counselling – the selection and preparation of helpers, the setting for the service, the advertising, initial contacts and follow-up procedures, confidentiality, competence and funding. It is these that cause many of the continuing headaches.

In essence, within the structure provided by an agency, counsellors offer help to people with emotional problems, through personal contact, by telephone or by letter, by giving time and attention. They give undivided attention to clients, struggling to enter into their world, to understand their problems better by feeling as closely as possible their pain or dilemmas, in the belief that at the very least a problem shared is a lightening of the burden and may well bring enormous relief.

The main resource for counsellors lies in their own qualities of warmth, perception and intuition, and in their skill at being, at one and the same time, deeply involved with their clients yet one step detached from them. For the client, this experience may seem strange and distant, or may be akin to meeting up with a trusted old friend who gives sympathy and understanding and brings hope to a day of despair. For the counsellor, it is a matter of trying to stay on the boundary of being engaged with the client but not becoming involved.

Counselling is best thought of as a relationship, but a relationship with a purpose. One early text defines it as 'a definitely structured permissive relationship which allows the client to gain an understanding of himself to a degree which enables him to take positive steps in the light of his new orientation' (Rogers 1942: 18). Basic to this way of thinking is the belief, well expressed by Bowlby (1969), that when an individual is isolated he may well be anxious, scared or emotionally stuck, but when experiencing the security of a close relationship with someone else he may become free to face changes in himself. What is needed is a positive attachment to someone else, a secure base from which to explore.

The necessary characteristics of what Bowlby (1969) terms this 'positive attachment figure' have been suggested as

> someone who will become familiar . . . with whom emotional issues can be raised; who is reliable and trustworthy; who can survive and acknowledge anger and failure on his part and that of his client; who is good enough . . . who can encourage the client's own efforts; who can share and cooperate; who can leave in a way which is not too traumatic.
>
> (Mattison and Sinclair 1979: 244)

An alternative way of understanding counselling is by analysis of what counsellors actually do. This describes counselling as the use of specific personal and relational tools or skills. These skills include 'those of forming an understanding relationship with clients, and skills focussed on helping them to change specific aspects of their feeling, thinking and behaviour' (Nelson-Jones 1983: 3).

These two aspects of counselling are complementary. There are skills to be learnt and knowledge to acquire, but of prime importance is the natural ability to form positive relationships, those qualities which have been identified as 'genuineness, accurate empathy and non-possessive warmth' (Truax and Carkhuff 1967). Counselling is primarily an art. The skill of agencies lies in selecting those who are naturals at the art, those who Balint (1964) described as having 'green fingers'. The voluntary sector relies mainly on these artists, and the training frequently focuses much more on closely supervised experience than on academic study.

The voluntary agencies aim at forming small groups of counsellors and other workers in which they can gain mutual support, can themselves be held in an emotional sense, find an identity and be supervised. Bearing other people's distress causes pressure for counsellors, and they themselves need their own means of continuing support. Counselling is not a haphazard process. Counsellors are fully aware of carrying, on behalf of their agency, the responsibility for the service they are providing for their clients. But the agency must shoulder its responsibility for supporting its workers, and ensuring, in the words of Cruse's training manual, that 'excessive demands are not made on the counsellor either by the bereaved client or by the organization' (Cruse 1987: Section 5.1).

DEVELOPING APPROACHES

Alongside the growth of counselling there has been an expanding literature on the subject. Carl Rogers was, and has remained, a seminal influence with his advocacy of a person-centred approach. He is associated with the concept of non-directiveness, but his disciples have tended to take this out of the context in which he first wrote. He was reacting against the prevailing tendency of the helping professions to use their authority in prescribing solutions for their clients. The professional helpers were not good at enabling their clients to talk about their own concerns and, with prompting, to work things out for themselves. Non-directiveness stressed the importance of listening before prescribing, of joint exploration with the client rather than authoritative solutions imposed on the client (Rogers 1961). Faced with this simple but quite dramatic change of emphasis in how to offer help with emotional problems, Rogerians have interpreted his teachings in exaggerated form by creating golden rules such as that of never offering advice and never giving directions.

In fact Rogers was advocating a flexible approach to the client, with the emphasis on client-centredness and on the vital importance of creating a safe environment. Many clients benefit from a *laissez-faire* or unstructured atmosphere. But other clients experience intolerable anxiety without an authoritative approach and fairly direct answers. The key is to respond, so Rogers says, in the way that you consider most appropriate for the client. The struggle is to distinguish what is right for the client from the response that most readily meets the counsellor's own needs and inclinations. For example, an experienced counsellor pointed out that she responded very differently in the two places she worked in. In her office in Chelsea she was more reflective, had longer contacts with her clients and felt appropriately non-directive for much of the time. By contrast, in Tower Hamlets she found herself being more authoritative, felt comfortable about giving advice and focused more directly on practical issues, with one-off interviews being the norm. She was the same person with the same understandings but she allowed herself to be used in quite different ways.

Client-centredness remains the basis for much of the counsellor training in the voluntary sector. However, relationships are a two-way process so the focus is not only on the clients but also on the feelings and reactions of the counsellors. Their training will therefore include an introspective aspect in which they are challenged to reflect on themselves and on the influences that have fashioned them. They are expected to become more conscious about their own strengths, and more aware of the losses they have suffered in their own lives and how those losses have influenced them. By so doing they can understand better their own bias and prejudices and the impact which they themselves make upon their clients. Counselling has been strongly influenced by the psychodynamic approach which emphasizes awareness of unconscious factors in human behaviour. Counsellors are unlikely to set out to delve deeply into a client's past; the focus is on the 'here and now' of present relationships. But, aware that the present is a product of the past, counsellors listen out for unresolved issues from the past which unconsciously intrude into and foul up present relationships. This can at times be something of a juggling act between the 'here and now' and the 'there and then', hopefully one on which the client and the counsellor work equally together.

In some agencies counsellors espouse some of the methods with strange-sounding names that advocate a more structured model of the helping process. Reality therapy (Glasser 1965), rational emotive therapy (Ellis 1977) and transactional analysis as propounded by Berne (1964) each teach a specific model for responding. Gestalt therapy (Perls 1969) advocates a holistic understanding of the interplay of mind, body and environmental factors. In contrast, the behavioural school seeks to change unacceptable behaviour without being concerned about the need to understand the causes of it (Skinner 1969). A widely used system in voluntary bodies is that of Egan (1986) who attempts to synthesize the person-centred and the behavioural approaches with a three-stage model of helping.

These and other schools were examined by Proctor (1978), who asked the practitioners what they considered to be the significant features in their practice. She found substantial differences and noted that controversy surfaces from time to time. But she concluded that the similarities outweighed the differences:

> One conclusion I draw from my experience is that it does not matter much what counsellors believe about the nature of human beings and society. It is the way that the counsellor is with a person that matters.
>
> (Proctor 1978: 14)

There is a common core which they all share – positive regard for the client and his autonomy, the giving of time and undivided attention, the importance of not exploiting the client and of treating him with respect and confidentiality.

These schools all view counselling as an intensely personal process.

In practice, most counselling takes place between one counsellor and one client. In addition, couple counselling occurs frequently in marital and conciliation counselling, and family counselling with several members of the same family is undertaken in some agencies. Group counselling is also practised occasionally where members can talk about their common experiences or problems and support each other. At times two or more counsellors may work jointly together with couples or groups. In some agencies counsellors will expect to be a source of information and give practical help and advice as part of the counselling task. In others the 'talking cure' will be the main or indeed the only therapeutic tool. The common thread is concern for individual clients.

GRASSROOTS GROWTH

At the same time as writers have been seeking to make sense of this new discipline, more agencies have been setting up in the voluntary sector, independently and pragmatically, to respond to new sufferers. New pioneers emerge and again find they 'must needs try'. As they do so they move imperceptibly into counselling.

Victim Support is a case in point. As crime rates soared in the 1970s there came a growing realization that victims of crime were often neglected and left to cope on their own with the shock and trauma resulting from their experience. In 1979 the National Association of Victim Support Services was formed to offer 'a comprehensive service of information and support to all victims of crime and to raise awareness of the effects of crime'.

Its early thrust was to recruit volunteers throughout Britain to visit and support victims of crime. Most of these crimes were burglaries, and visitors from Victim Support groups were trained to give sympathy and assurances that practical help could be available from a central office. The visitors called once, with possibly one follow-up call, but further contact was discouraged. This was a demonstration of society's concern. Many victims were grateful for the visit.

However the visitors soon found that some victims needed more time to talk through the circumstances of the crime – how and why it happened, what might have been done to prevent it and how to avoid a repetition. They had an urgent need to express their feelings of anger, surprise and distress, especially at the loss of treasured possessions or the sense of being violated by the break into their home.

One victim said:

> I hadn't realized how much all my bits and pieces meant to
> me. I always thought home was just a comfortable place to
> live in. Now I feel every knick-knack meant something special
> to me. So many have gone or been smashed, and I feel bereft.
> There's no point in claiming on the insurance because noth-
> ing can replace them.

She began to mention her possessions one by one and to say what
each one meant to her. As she got round to describing the last
present her husband gave her before he died, she could no longer
fight back her tears. 'He was a good man in many ways but we
were never what you would call close. That clock was the nearest
he came to giving me a personal present.' The visitor was becoming
increasingly aware that the loss of the articles was opening the
floodgates of feelings about other losses, and she became uneasy.
'The worst part' continued her client, 'was that the thief got into
my bedroom and rifled through all my underclothes. You see I've
always been a very private person. Even he', she said, referring to
her husband in a way which showed she had already accepted the
visitor into the intimacy of her thoughts, 'even he never saw me
undress. We didn't do that sort of thing in those days.' The visitor
was trying to calm her own panic, thinking she might be becoming involved in something too deep for her to handle; and she was
wondering where she might suggest this elderly woman could go
for more intensive help. But any thought of going elsewhere for
counselling was brushed aside. 'I couldn't talk to anyone like I've
talked to you. It's been such a relief. You're so understanding.
Please come back again when I've got myself together a bit.'
    Some victims, like this woman, found that the real help lay in
just having someone to talk to about their experience. Others wanted
practical help or advice about insurance or compensation. Training
for the volunteers was extended to make them knowledgeable about
claims for compensation. Particular challenges were presented by
crimes of violence. People who had suffered physical or sexual assaults, and families of murder victims, needed more time to talk
through what had happened. Gradually specialist training and
supervision had to be provided for the experienced volunteers
working on these cases. Guidelines were drawn up for what
was recognized to be a particularly stressful form of counselling
(Victim Support 1991).
    The visitors were now forming much more intensive relationships

with some of their clients than originally envisaged, and Victim Support encouraged contact with these victims to be maintained over a longer period of time. It also became apparent that personal support could not be limited to the immediate aftermath of the crime but might be necessary over the often protracted period of remand and court appearances of the accused. Volunteers found they could be useful in accompanying victims to court, preparing them for the ordeal of giving evidence and 'debriefing' them after their appearances in the witness box. Coming face to face with the defendant reactivated the trauma. The court proceedings forced them to relive all the horrors of the crime.

Victim Support thus came under pressure to develop in further directions. In 1991 it established new posts in court buildings where support and counselling could be available for victims and their families who had not sought help before. It was also encouraged to extend its help to cover car thefts, which had not been its original practice. The police pointed out that many car thefts resulted in serious accidents and no support existed for the casualties. And if those victims came into its remit, why not give help to any victims of accidents on the road?

Once Victim Support was acknowledged to be expert in understanding issues arising for victims, its staff were called in to serve on working parties on various other aspects of crime and violence. So, for instance, a multi-disciplinary working party on domestic violence concluded that extra help should be given to people abused by their partners, and who better to assist and befriend these victims than Victim Support?

Voluntary organizations are subject to these sorts of pressure to extend the boundaries of help they provide and take on more complex work. After fifty years in marriage guidance, the NMGC changed its name to Relate, as a more accurate description of the range of its clientele in an age of widespread cohabitation, divorce and remarriage. Simultaneously the Marriage Research Centre, based in Central Middlesex Hospital, became One-plus-One! Cruse which began thirty years ago running social clubs for widows now deals with all aspects of bereavement.

Where do these pressures to extend the scope of work come from? A study of this growth in Cruse identified two main processes in operation (Stanners 1987). The external pressures were from those potential clients and referrers who had problems akin to those dealt with by Cruse, and who referred people to Cruse as having the most relevant expertise available. Counsellors and supervisors had to learn by extending their experience.

The internal pressures were equally strong. They came from the counsellors who thirsted to gain greater skill and understanding by meeting new challenges and having further training opportunities; and from the professional advisers who sought to research other aspects of bereavement. The latter are particularly significant, concludes Stanners. 'It is the powerful executive role which professionals tend to assume in the management of voluntary organisations, which makes the professional influence a major one on policy changes' (Stanners 1987: 116). Under this professional direction, there has been a progression in Cruse's remit. It has extended from social clubs to counselling; from being only widows to accepting widowers, and then offering services to all bereaved by death; and finally extending its sphere of interest to include disasters affecting whole communities, both in peace and in war.

Voluntary groups find it hard to resist these pressures. The organizations are free of statutory constraints and so are free to innovate. The danger is that their resources are stretched too far and that they overreach themselves. But, faced with new cries of pain and injustice, the volunteers of today, like the missionaries of old, 'must needs try'. What starts as a step into the unknown, a shoulder to cry on perhaps, soon has to draw on the understandings and responses of counselling, often long before the helpers have accepted that they are counsellors. The art becomes more and more technical. The amateur becomes the expert.

In its train comes the process of making a formal system of counselling. Other forms of help come to be seen as less effective; counselling acquires greater status and prominence. Counselling becomes institutionalized, so to speak. The Westminster Pastoral Foundation's history shows this at work. It was formed within the churches to advance pastoral care and counselling. These were conceived as the informal and formal ways of giving care. The formal way soon took precedence. Looking back at its first two decades, Black (1991) noted how quickly the pastoral care part of its remit took second place to counselling.

When the Foundation began, pastoral care was an ill-defined aspect of a pastor's work, with no clear boundaries. It was seen as just one aspect of the multi-faceted role of a minister of religion. In no way was it a specialist activity. In contrast, counselling was coming to be well recognized as a specialism. It had definable aims and quasi-professional status. So practitioners were quicker to sign up for counselling courses, and trainers felt more confident about providing courses in counselling skills. Workers and agencies were much less keen about courses in pastoral care. So, while pastoral care remained undeveloped, counselling grew by leaps and bounds. The Foundation later became the centre of a network of independent general counselling agencies throughout the country.

As we shall see in later chapters, counselling comes in various forms, from treatment which is defined and regulated to what has been aptly termed 'counselling on the hoof'. In Britain counselling now occupies centre-stage, with well-focused training available, with possibilities of measuring its effectiveness and with counsellors, whether paid or voluntary, acquiring a quasi-professional status. In the next chapter I turn the spotlight on how voluntary groups function as counselling agencies.

TWO

Voluntary agencies

THE ROLE OF VOLUNTARY AGENCIES

A young clergyman was called upon to conduct the funeral of a 14-year-old girl who had killed herself when her menstruation had started. She had not known what was happening to her and had no one to ask about it (Keir 1986: 154). The curate was deeply moved and was determined to prevent other such tragedies. He hit on the idea of setting up an emergency telephone number which desperate people could call. He and his colleagues answered the calls.

As the number of calls grew, however, he enlisted the assistance of some of his congregation to give tea and comfort to the telephone callers who had responded to his invitation to come to talk to him in person. Before long he realized that the care and attention that these volunteers were giving to the callers was as valuable as any advice he could give them. Thus was the Samaritans born. Now, nearly 50 years later, the Samaritans offers a nation-wide service by telephone helpline, drop-in contact and ongoing befriending and counselling.

The Samaritans has a strong sense of purpose or mission. Its aim is not just to help troubled individuals but to make a significant impact on the suicide rate in Britain. It cites with pride the fact that when the number of Samaritans branches was increasing there was a steady decline in the suicide rate which was not echoed in other countries where no such organization existed (Keir 1986: 155).

Like the Samaritans, many other caring organizations in the voluntary sector have a mission. They often have a clear ideology, sometimes enshrined in a set of principles. This may be based on a strong sense of injustice, as it often is in women's groups or with

ethnic minorities. It may spring from a shared religious belief or
from a common set of values about, for instance, family life. There
may be tensions within the organizations as to what priority to give
to helping individuals and what to pressing for educational or social
reform.

These tensions are worked out in various ways. Charity laws
forbid agencies that are charities taking part in political action, so
counselling agencies that have charitable status are constrained in
campaigning activities. The boundary between legitimate educational
initiatives and campaigning is by no means clear. One solution is
to set up separate organizations. This happens, for instance, with
abortion. This is a very emotive area to be involved in. It is impossible for workers counselling girls with unwanted pregnancies not
to have strong views about abortion laws. The pregnancy advisory
services are charities and therefore cannot themselves campaign for
reform. Political action thus falls to the non-charitable bodies on
either side of the issue, the Abortion Law Reform Association and
the Society for the Protection of Unborn Children.

'Values are part of the essence of voluntary organizations', comments Handy (1981). He identifies two sets of values – the 'how'
values and the 'why' values. The 'why' values are the rationale
for the organization, the shared mission, the vision that inspired the
pioneers and now sustain the work of the group. The 'how' values
are the means for carrying out that mission.

In the organizations we are studying here, the 'how' values are
primarily expressed in counselling. Counsellors are motivated by
their own value system, however neutral they aspire to be in their
attitude to their clients. Halmos (1965: 104) noted this dilemma
many years ago.

> At its lowest estimate the counsellor cannot sustain the activity
> of healing another . . . and avoid communicating the idea that
> concern for the welfare of others is worthwhile! . . . The whole
> performance is inevitably personal, and biased in some most
> important sense. The truth lies not in disowning that bias, but
> rather acting on it with full awareness and frank admission.

The organization's 'why' values may be set out in a mission statement or a set of principles. These may change from time to time,
as the original vision of the pioneers becomes modified or the social
environment changes. Such changes can be clearly identified during the fifty years' history of the National Marriage Guidance Council,
changes which contributed to its renaming itself Relate in the late
1980s.

NMGC altered its official 'Principles' four times over the years. In 1943 it boldly stated the following:

> The right foundation of the family unit is permanent monog-
> amous marriage which alone provides satisfactory conditions
> for the birth and upbringing of children, for the expression of
> the function of sex and for a secure relationship between man
> and woman.

By 1968 the Principles had become Objectives and were much less dogmatic. 'The Council is concerned primarily with marriage and family relationships and believes that the well-being of society is dependent on the stability of marriage'. In 1983 a new statement declared: 'The Council is concerned with marriage and with family and personal relationships and believes that the quality of these relationships is fundamental to the well-being of society'. Four years later its Common Purpose Statement added: 'the Council cannot be committed to any one sectional, social, political, cultural or religious view of marriage'.

This shift in its value system over the years is reflected in other ways. It has meant a change in the terminology in use in the organ-ization. NMGC thought of itself originally as a 'movement', as have the hospice movement and other bodies subsequently. Gradually its emphasis changed to that of service provider, and the word 'movement' fell into disfavour. This shift from movement to service provider has been well charted in marriage guidance (Lewis *et al.* 1992: 8), and can be seen in other voluntary bodies. A movement is characterized by having 'values to promote'; a service provider thinks in terms of having 'objectives to achieve'. There is a conse-quent move away from attracting 'members to affirm those values' to using 'personnel to implement the objectives'. Similarly there is a change in how helpers are perceived. Movements are geared to soliciting 'a donation of service of care in furtherance of ideals'; service providers make use of 'paid and routine application of skills'. So this gradual process away from being a movement marks a significant shift from being 'amateur and unpaid' to being providers of a service which aspires to be 'professional and paid'.

These distinctions are important in the understanding of counsel-ling in the voluntary sector. Counselling is in transition. Many different conceptions exist about what constitutes counselling, based on a variety of value systems. Voluntary agencies occupy many points on the continuum between what is thought of in amateur terms as a movement, and a service that claims to have professional standards.

Value systems also need to be understood because the counselling culture may sit uneasily within the wider culture of the agency. This tension is apparent, for instance, in the Catholic Marriage Advisory Council (CMAC), formed in 1946 to function within the ethos and practice of the Catholic Church; indeed, for over 30 years its officers were priests appointed by the Catholic hierarchy. Yet the counsellors, although all practising Catholics, were trained in non-directive methods which resulted in the thrust of their counselling often being at variance with the Church's official line, particularly on contraception.

As we examine in this chapter the formation of different types of voluntary counselling organizations, it becomes apparent how varied are their 'how' and 'why' values. These values are not only important in themselves, but also act as the magnet which draws volunteers of all sorts to offer to be of service.

THE VOLUNTARY ETHOS

Voluntary organizations attract large numbers of helpers. It is estimated that two-fifths of the population is in membership of charitable organizations, and about one in six undertake voluntary work (Gerard 1983: 149).

These volunteers are not drawn proportionately from all sectors of the community, however. They come predominately from middle-aged people with school-age families, the upper social groups and the better educated. One study of their characteristics shows that these volunteers are reflective in disposition, more trusting, more altruistic and less materialistic than others not so involved. The majority express religious convictions and strict moral attitudes, and find greater meaning in life and enjoy greater levels of psychological well-being than non-volunteers.

The motivation of volunteers is complex. Many reasons for volunteering have been identified. Sharrott differentiated 'instrumental' and 'moral and normative' categories. The instrumental reasons are those that give tangible benefits in return. Those volunteering may be looking for friendship or for an activity in retirement. They may see it as a means of enhancing job prospects, or as an interesting leisure pursuit. They may be women who want a substitute for employment while they are still engaged in family obligations. The second category are those who volunteer for moral and normative reasons. These include people who have a strong sense of social duty, and those who have ideals about ways of neighbourhood

living or for whom it is an expression of religious beliefs. Also
included in this category are those who consciously or unconsciously
are seeking to appease guilt (Poulton 1988: 22).

Counselling agencies are familiar with two other reasons for
volunteering. Many mid-life volunteers are searching for a possible
new career and wish to test themselves as voluntary counsellors.
Less welcome are those volunteers whose offer of help disguises a
strong need for personal therapy. For selectors, as we will explore
in a later chapter, those belonging in this last category constitute a
challenge. Their unconscious motivation may be strong, and it may
be well disguised. Before being considered for selection they may
first have to accept the need to be a client, and receive personal
help.

Voluntary bodies tend to become collections of like-minded people.
Campaigning organizations need different types of volunteer from
those that see their main role as providing practical aid or advice
and counselling services for the troubled and disadvantaged. These
are two different styles of social action, and both are necessary.
As far as widows are concerned, the National Association of Widows
and Cruse Bereavement Care both set out to help. The former fills
the campaigning role of lobbying for increased widows' pensions,
while Cruse provides counselling for individuals. Similarly for gay
clients, the Albany Trust and National Friend provide counselling
services, while the lobbying for gay rights is done by the Campaign
for Homosexual Equality.

The relative importance of social action and personal service varies
from age to age. A decade which has produced equal opportunities
legislation, Citizens' Charters and the Freedom of Information Act
has made a subtle shift of emphasis in the counselling room.
Counsellors are now less inclined to encourage their clients to learn
how to adapt to circumstances that seem intolerable; they are more
ready to give clients confidence to take action to change those
circumstances.

It is important that volunteers find their way to the type of organization that best suits their talents and interests. Increasing numbers are guided in the right direction by local Volunteer Bureaux.
Giving voluntary service meets the needs of individuals to have
their own personal sense of purpose, to belong to a corporate entity
and to make a significant individual contribution to society. The
skill of management lies in ensuring that these needs of volunteers
mesh with the actual task of the agency and do not become paramount. In other words, the means must not become the end. It is
all too easy for corporate organizations to become institutionalized

and unresponsive to change. When the organizations are mainly staffed by volunteers this danger is enhanced.

Some people maintain that no voluntary organizations ought to remain in existence for more than ten years. By that time, they contend, either the objective for which the organization was set up will have been achieved; or the mission will have been found to be flawed in some way, and the pioneering group will have ceased to exist. The objective will be shown to have been achieved if the injustice has been righted; or if the social need has been clearly demonstrated, and an effective service for responding to it has been created. If so, such service should pass from the voluntary sector and be provided on a regular basis by statutory bodies.

In Britain, however, this has not happened. Voluntary bodies which proved their point decades ago still continue to flourish. To some extent this is linked to the issue of motivation of volunteers. But it is also true that the members of these organizations are proud of their achievements. They naturally become possessive of what they have created, and are loath to pass it on to statutory services. They fear, with justification, that their special cause would have to fight for priority among the many demands on the social services' pot of gold. The government in its turn is in no hurry to take on extra commitments, and may well genuinely believe that a particular client group can best continue to be served in its traditional way by voluntary endeavour.

The statutory social services were subject to major restructuring in 1970. New comprehensive social services departments were set up. The report that recommended these changes identified three roles for the voluntary sector (Seebohm 1968). One was the pioneer role discussed above. Recent examples of such pioneering are those concerned with mediating in disputes between neighbours; and groups for grandparents to help in the understanding of issues about access to grandchildren. In addition Seebohm envisaged the voluntary sector would continue to provide some specialist services. Many of the groups concerned with disabilities fall into this category. Finally, the report argued that there was a continuing role for alternative services. These might be particularly for work which commanded little popular support, such as with client groups which were felt to be 'undeserving' – discharged prisoners, drug addicts and vagrants – or which raised particularly sensitive issues – such as gay rights and racial equality. One commentator has coined the phrase 'exiles in our midst' to describe these categories (Gerard 1983: 40).

These types of organizational role still exist. They can often be identified by the way the agency came into being. There were three main ways: some began as self-help groups; some were brought into being by a group of citizens concerned about a new problem which they had encountered; some were formed as an offshoot of an existing body. In the next three sections, I identify the main features of these three groups, and give a detailed example of an organization in each category.

SELF-HELP GROUPS

People facing a crisis or new situation often feel the need to meet with others in the same predicament. They may be in a state of shock after hearing bad news. They may feel panic in the face of a future which suddenly seems empty. They may simply not know where to turn for practical help. Their first reaction may be to wonder how others cope with the same crisis. An advertisement in a local paper, or a helpful social worker or minister, or a chance meeting in an out-patients' clinic may uncover others with a similar urge to get together.

In such a way a group of Rastafarian women began meeting in a church vestry in Camberwell. They came together for mutual support in a social environment which they experienced as strange and hostile. As problems were aired, natural leaders emerged to whom new members of the group turned for advice. There were no clear roles or structure, but social contact, befriending and counselling helped them learn from each other. Its success was seen in the growth in membership. The curtain which cordonned off one corner of the vestry was taken down. The group took over the whole vestry.

Another self-help group is the Duchesne Muscular Dystrophy group. Duchesne muscular dystrophy afflicts boys only and is diagnosed when they are around three years old. The news has to be broken to the parents that the prognosis is that within twenty years the child will die. This devastating news leaves parents with the twin tasks of helping their son develop as fully as possible in the intervening years, while preparing themselves and all their family for the certainty of premature death. Practical and financial information is needed. Where are mobility aids available? Which schools are most suitable? There are new aspects of parenting to consider. How is it best to talk to the other children in the family about what is happening to their brother? There are concerns to talk through. How will the family adjust itself to cope with a handicapped son? And there are unanswerable questions which keep recurring. Why has this happened to this particular family?

Meeting in a group with other similar parents helps air and share such difficulties. Sometimes one partner does not feel able to talk openly in front of other couples, however sympathetic they are. Sometimes the need or the hurt is so great that one parent or one couple monopolizes all the attention of the group to the detriment of the other members. Individuals may need more time to talk on their own. Gradually some of the more experienced members, generally those furthest removed from the immediate shock of the diagnosis, find themselves supporting these more needy parents, and ask for training to help them become better counsellors.

The families who lived in and around London were fortunate to be able to meet in this particular group. But others were in remote parts of Britain where it was not possible to meet with others. The telephone numbers of the original parents in the group were printed in a newsletter, and an unofficial helpline was formed. Practical information was sought by telephone, but increasingly the calls were from desperate parents, shattered at the news and wondering how they were going to cope. The members of the early self-help group had to draw on their own personal experience. There was no one else available to give the time and understanding required. Gradually a small but essential service of advice, befriending and counselling was built up out of the original group.

A similar development, now much further advanced, took place among a number of parents who had suffered the death of a child. A priest in the Midlands encouraged bereaved parents to get in touch with each other. They called themselves the Society of Compassionate Friends. That was the beginning of a nation-wide organization. Now known just as Compassionate Friends, membership is restricted to parents who have experienced this loss, whatever the age of their offspring. Members can meet in local groups or at the national annual conference. From the membership befrienders are selected and trained to visit newly bereaved parents. Though the title 'counsellor' is eschewed, the befrienders are given a thorough preparation in how to listen and relate to those they visit. Understanding and sharing the grief are the core of this help. Central to it is the belief that only those who have suffered a similar loss can fully know what those they are visiting are going through. There is, too, a firmly held belief that those offered help will only feel the help is credible if the helper also has experienced the death of his or her own child.

This sense of a shared traumatic experience creates a powerful bond in any self-help group. Those who join the group find a support which may include both social interaction with like-minded

people, and, in counselling terms, the opportunity through individual contact to try to make sense of their bereavement. But not
all bereaved parents want to meet with others experiencing the
same loss. Some find it irksome rather than comforting to hear
about the grief of others. Some are so overwhelmed by grief that
they can only feel that no other grief can compare with their own.
A self-help group is not for everyone.

Cruse Bereavement Care, which started solely as a self-help group,
has developed to meet a variety of needs. It still has a self-help
ethos. Bereaved people become members, and receive a monthly
chronicle that consists of articles, comment and information about
bereavement. All branches run social groups where bereaved people
can meet others similarly bereaved. But now therapeutic groups are
also held for more focused discussion, for example for people who
have been bereaved by the suicide by a relative. Additionally, counsellors are recruited and trained to help those who ask for individual attention. They visit the bereaved at home or offer them
counselling in central offices.

These developments have not been without their difficulties.
Indeed, Chris Stanners (1987: 121) comments on the ambiguity
that continues to exist within the organization:

> Cruse as a counselling organization and Cruse as a Widows'
> Club reflect a different perception of need . . . between be-
> reavement perceived as a life-state and bereavement seen as
> a transitory condition; between the levers of change and the
> countervailing conservative forces.

Nowhere is this ambiguity more apparent than in different perceptions about what fits people to become bereavement counsellors. Some believe, like Compassionate Friends, that all counsellors
should have experienced a close bereavement. The official policy in
Cruse, however, is to recruit a range of people who are sensitive
and open to the grief of others. Some have been bereaved by the
death of a friend or relative, and over the years have come to terms
with that experience. Most have suffered some form of loss, and
have grown in understanding through that loss. Some have worked
professionally with dying people and their families. The belief is
that all these experiences can help in understanding the pain of
bereavement.

But that is not necessarily so. Though counsellors may gain in
understanding from having experienced a close trauma themselves,
such an experience can be so powerful that it may actually prove
to be a barrier to understanding the grief of others. Cruse therefore

has a policy of not selecting those who have suffered a close be-reavement within the previous two years, on the grounds that, in counselling others, the helpers' own trauma may be revived and may too strongly influence how they hear and respond to the client's story. Those selected as counsellors recognize that there are common features in all bereavement yet must bear in mind in counselling that all grief is personal and unique.

The pros and cons of recruiting counsellors who have personal experience of the clients' difficulties are debated in other voluntary settings. Should counsellors in gay and lesbian groups be homosexual? In which case, should heterosexuals only be counselled by heterosexuals (Sketchley 1991: 240)? Is the experience of having been raped an essential requirement to being a counsellor in a Rape Crisis centre?

These are important questions, though there are no comprehensive answers to them. Counsellors are the sum total of their individual experiences. They must be able to draw from those experiences, yet not make assumptions from them about other people's experiences. They must be informed by their own past and present, yet be sufficiently detached from those influences. Wisdom lies in knowing their strengths and being aware of their blindspots, but not being dominated by them. One mother became a bereavement counsellor some years after the death of her only daughter. She anticipated that she would be able to be of assistance to other parents facing a similar loss. Six years later she confided that she now felt confident as a counsellor to help in most types of loss, and she was indeed an excellent counsellor. But she still could not trust herself to counsel families over the death of a child.

SPECIALIST SERVICES

The voluntary sector provides many specialist services. Some of these go back a long way. The original organizations, Barnados and the Shaftesbury Society, continue their work with children. They have been supplemented by others such as the Children's Society, and the National Children's Homes, all of which increasingly provide specialist services for particular types of disadvantaged child. In the current contract culture, much of the work of these societies is done on contract to local authority social services departments who depend upon their specialist expertise.

Other organizations provide specialist services but remain largely independent of statutory control. Marriage guidance has come a

long way since the early desire of their counsellors to 'needs try'.
Now known as Relate (except in London, which retains the title
Marriage Guidance Council, and in Scotland which has its Marriage
Counselling Service), its counsellors undergo a well-established
system of training. This consists of a series of residential sessions at
its national college in Rugby, with supervised practice in their own
local settings. Centrally organized selection of counsellors is still
considered to be of paramount importance.

Counsellors work with individuals or couples, basing their approach on a client-centred philosophy and drawing on psychodynamic understandings. The counsellor starts by listening to the
client describing the problem, and the gradual unfolding of the difficulties begins to throw new light on them. Talking becomes itself
the first stage in the alleviation of the pressures, with the counsellor
helping to clarify issues through comments or questions. Together
client and counsellor may explore further aspects of the problem
or plan future action. The diagnosis and the healing process take
place gradually and simultaneously.

Marriage counsellors work sometimes in pairs, though mostly
they work individually. They might see one or both of the partners,
singly or together. In fact there is a steady growth in the number
of couples who both attend for counselling – in 1975 only 19% of
interviews involved both partners; by 1982 the number had risen
to 27%; in 1986 to 39%; and by 1992 to over 40% (NMGC annual
reports). When clients attend on their own, counsellors work in the
conviction that they can influence the marriage by seeing only one
partner.

A further specialist development took place in the 1970s when a
service was started based on behavioural techniques for couples
with specific sexual dysfunctions, staffed by experienced marriage
counsellors. This was based on a dramatically new approach. Whereas
over the years counsellors had moved away from the medical
procedure of diagnosis, treatment and cure, the sexual dysfunction
programme returned to that model. In this specialist project, based
on the work of Masters and Johnson (1966) and Kaplan (1979),
counsellors adopted the title of 'therapist', worked in clinics, conducted diagnostic sessions and prescribed firm treatment plans.

The sex therapy emphasis was primarily educational. Couples
had to attend together and were guided through a relearning programme about sexual functioning. This therapeutic approach was
markedly different from the traditional Rogerian counselling, yet
the two approaches were developed in tandem. The sex therapists
are all recruited from the ranks of experienced counsellors. Couple

counselling is held to be an important component of sex therapy, and practitioners need to be flexible. Care has to be taken to ensure that couples end up with the help that is most suited to their needs.

Conciliation is a later adaptation of marital counselling. This is work with couples who are separating or intending to divorce, in order to help them make decisions about their family relationships for the future. Conciliation and mediation services were established in many places in the 1980s, some within the aegis of civil courts and some independently; some new, and some linked with established marriage counselling or probation services. The National Family Conciliation Council was formed as an umbrella body in 1982.

In conciliation a clear focus of a different sort is required. Decisions have to be made within a limited time-scale about the future care of the children. The parents are often at loggerheads themselves. Counsellors can find themselves in the role of referee. At times they may have to cope with underlying resentment from the couple, who may experience them as interfering with their parental autonomy (Clulow and Vincent 1987). The skill of counselling in conciliation is to ensure that both parents, however much at war they are, feel they have made the arrangements together for the child care, and are therefore committed to see those arrangements are carried out as agreed.

OFFSHOOT AGENCIES

I choose the term 'offshoot' to describe a third main group of voluntary counselling agencies. These are bodies that are set up by established organizations to fill a specific need which has become apparent in their normal services. Examples of these organizations are mental health departments, churches and hospitals.

The Hospice movement is one case in point. Hospices have become a major feature of the voluntary sector, since Cicely Saunders founded St Christopher's Hospice in Sydenham, south London, in 1967 (du Boulay 1984). Each hospice is independent. The movement is served by an information centre based at St Christopher's, which is purely advisory and has no managerial authority. Several of the hospices have been started by hospitals or religious bodies. The Princess Alice Hospice for dying children at Tolworth Court was an offshoot of Great Ormond Street Children's Hospital. In contrast, Helen House in Oxford was founded through the individual inspiration of Mother Francis Domenica.

As a follow-up to the care they provide for dying patients, several hospices started to give after-care to families of relatives who died in their care. They recruited voluntary counsellors for this offshoot activity, to undertake bereavement visiting. Many of them now have well-trained teams of volunteers visiting homes and giving counselling to families of relatives who are terminally ill or have died.

Teams of counsellors have been formed in other similar settings. For instance, the staff of an infertility unit in one of the London teaching hospitals became aware of the lack of follow-up help for some of their couples. They were particularly conscious of the pain felt by couples who successfully conceived but then had their hopes dashed by the discovery of foetal abnormality. They formed a group to provide counselling for couples facing decisions about termination, and support for those who opted for an abortion. From this beginning grew an agency known as SAFTA (Support Following Termination after Foetal Abnormality). As the couples so affected come from a widely dispersed area, much of the counselling is provided by letter and telephone contact.

Another example of a counselling service set up as an offshoot body from a medical service is the Isis centre in Oxford (Oldfield 1983). It was an extension into the community of the psychiatric service provided by Littlemore Hospital and financed largely by the Regional Health Authority. It has a shop front on the street and aims to make itself accessible to the general public. It successfully attracts clients attending on their own initiative, as well as those encouraged to refer themselves by friends, doctors or professional advisers. The counselling team is now a mix of volunteers drawn from medical and non-medical settings.

The Catholic Church has a wide-ranging social services programme which provides counselling in various guises, either through the welfare work of the Society of St Vincent de Paul or through the more specialist counselling service of the Catholic Marriage Advisory Council. CMAC has a network of over 100 centres, linked with local Catholic churches, yet jealous of its independence. As well as providing marital counselling, the counsellors run courses for engaged and newly married couples, groups for children and parents in family life and sex education, and work with medical specialists on family planning, and problems of infertility and non-consummation.

In some parts of Britain local authority social services departments have set up counselling agencies which are independently managed but almost entirely financed by the local authority. Open

Door in Feltham is one such example. It was started in 1982 for 'people who are distressed or isolated'. Originally financed with an Urban Aid grant, the social services department took over funding when the original grant expired and it is now part of the local authority's Care in the Community programme. Open Door is staffed by a project co-ordinator and a counselling co-ordinator. It offers information, counselling and befriending through a drop-in centre, groupwork and individual counselling. Some of its clients hear of the service independently and refer themselves. Others come via the social services department and include discharged psychiatric patients, long-term unemployed people and those with mental health problems. A special group is also run for Asian women.

The counsellors are all volunteers, many of whom start with Open Door on placement from a counselling course and continue to undertake half a day's counselling on a voluntary basis each week. Supervision in small groups for all counsellors is provided by the agency, with professional supervisors employed on a sessional basis. All clients are given an assessment interview by the counselling co-ordinator.

Because of the wide range of clients, the Management Committee has decided to concentrate its resources on short-term counselling. It has laid down a structure by which counsellors offer clients an initial contract lasting up to six weekly sessions, with the possibility of renewing the contract for two further blocks of six sessions. If a counsellor wishes to extend counselling beyond these 18 sessions with any client, permission has to be given by the counselling co-ordinator who is able to approve a further six sessions in exceptional circumstances.

This decision to offer time-limited counselling has been made as a way of determining priorities. It ensures that long waiting lists do not build up. It focuses the attention of counsellor and client on problem-solving. However, it narrows the type of help provided and is a reminder that there is limited autonomy for an agency which is set up to meet the needs of a parent body and continues to be funded by that body. The social services department monitors the performance of Open Door closely. It is sensitive of the need for crisis counselling for many of those who are the responsibility of the statutory services. The social workers need to be convinced that their statutory clients are not losing out at Open Door in favour of self-referred clients who may benefit from long-term counselling. The agency has to guard against this possibility, especially as the counsellors themselves are likely to find it more satisfying to work with those clients who refer themselves.

LOCAL GROUPS

The impetus to set up a voluntary organization generally springs spontaneously from one particular locality. A need is perceived and a group comes together to do something about it. For instance, Crossroads was conceived in Rugby to provide care for one young man in a wheelchair. It has now grown into the Association of Crossroads Care Attendant Schemes and is still based there. Similarly Stepfamily originated with a small group of step-parents meeting in Cambridge; the Miscarriage Association began in Ossett.

These beginnings are generally followed by similar initiatives in other places. In time a network of similar bodies is built up nationwide. The impetus for new branches then tends to change. The headquarters of that network establishes a procedure for opening new branches. It may then take the initiative for planning to develop in particular towns or areas, or will insist that groups that are hoping to start a branch make application at an early stage to head office. The spread of branches throughout the country can thus be centrally monitored.

The extent of these networks varies. Victim Support reported in its 1992 *Annual Report* that it had achieved total national coverage with some 300 schemes. Stepfamily and the Stillbirth and Neo-natal Death Society are two of several organizations still actively trying to achieve a nation-wide spread of local groups. Cruse, which in 1992 had 180 groups, was also far short of national coverage. Indeed, it had a waiting list of over 60 applications requesting to set up local branches in other places.

Some local groups decide to remain independent. A bereavement group was set up in a town in the North-East of England at the instigation of a doctor, a priest and one or two bereaved people. Originally they applied for membership of Cruse. The response to that application was long delayed, and the group had meanwhile made a lot of progress. It had worked out its own programme, selected potential counsellors, and, with the help of a nearby branch, provided a basic training course for them.

The committee then weighed up the arguments for joining a national umbrella organization. Membership would mean receiving regular mailing of information, opportunities to participate in central training events and conferences, advice from headquarters in times of crisis and the sense of solidarity in belonging to a nationally recognized network.

However, these advantages carried obligations. There was the financial one of paying a membership fee; and a secretarial one of responding to correspondence from headquarters and to requests for statistics and information. Furthermore, there was a geographical problem as many of the events they would be invited to attend were located many miles away and would involve costly journeys.

This particular group decided that, on balance, it was more advantageous to remain independent. The national networks based in London seemed remote in every sense from their local northern culture and issues. The group realized that it would need to guard against excessive parochialism by keeping open the lines of communication with other relevant bodies. After working as a steering committee for three years, the group's members were confident they could manage on their own.

ETHNIC GROUPS

Counselling is a phenomenon of Western culture. It flourishes in North America, Europe and Australasia, in societies where basic needs of food, health and shelter are largely met. Maslow (1970) contends that human beings have a hierarchy of needs, and that it is only when personal security and comfort are obtained that individuals are able to concern themselves with solving emotional problems and striving towards self-actualization. Counselling is primarily concerned with emotional issues and personal formation. Those are very low priorities in parts of the world where hunger and poverty abound.

In developed countries, counselling has its limitations. It is not a cure-all. Many people still need immediate practical help, money or information. Others are unable to conceive that talking about their problems can bring relief. Early research into casework offered in a lower socio-economic area of London showed misunderstandings between worker and client. Mayer and Timms (1970) reported that many clients felt their caseworker failed to give them the help they required. They only returned to her because she proposed further sessions which they hoped would bring help, and anyway she was 'such a nice lady'.

Brigid Proctor was working as a probation officer at the time of that research. She reflects that the psychodynamic 'shoe' with which she had been fitted in her training never seemed quite practical for her clients. 'I often tried to fit their varied feet to the shoe, rather than really seeing their feet', Proctor (1991: 50) concluded.

Failure of communication in counselling takes several forms. In those instances it stemmed from differences of class and education between worker and client. There was an imbalance between how the agencies and their workers saw themselves, and how the clients saw them. More obviously there may be differences of race, culture and language. None of these difficulties should be underestimated. Many people find it difficult to talk about their emotional problems. It is doubly difficult to explain them when talking to someone who does not speak one's first language, nor understand the cultural roots in which these emotions are experienced.

Cultural practices complicate matters further. Misunderstandings over seeking help can arise in many ways. In Britain counsellors are taught the importance of gaining eye contact with clients. For many Asians, to look people straight in the eye implies extreme familiarity and is considered quite improper with strangers.

In traditional Asian communities women do not go out un-accompanied in public. In her study of non-English speaking Pathan women in Bradford, Currer (1983) noted that when women are ill their husbands go to consult the doctor on their behalf. One husband came back from the GP bearing a prescription for his wife. She assumed it was a prayer cure, so made it into a *tarwiz* or prayer neck-lace and wore it for a week. The outcome was that at the end of that week she was cured, but not in the way the doctor intended!

In many cultures helpers, be they medical or spiritual or just old and wise, are imbued with awesome powers of knowing and healing. The traditional helping process is often one in which the suppliant states the problem and the helper provides the remedy. This is far from the Western notion of clients and counsellors working together on the problem, with the helpers facilitating the clients in arriving at their own solutions through discussion.

Cultural differences mean that the helping process develops at various speeds and in a number of directions in agencies offering service to specific ethnic groups. The Asian Family Counselling Service illustrates this. The service sprang from the realization that the well-established marriage guidance agencies were not attracting clients from the immigrant community. For a while it was thought that the close family ties and customs in the extended Asian families coped adequately with any relationship difficulties. However, evid-ence of tensions surfaced, particularly in the younger generation caught in the clash of cultures between East and West, between parental mores and the environment of their upbringing. It was evident that the Asian community were unwilling or unable to turn for help to the MGC, which was white and English-speaking. An alternative was needed, some setting which Asians could identify with as their sort of place.

The Asian service was originally set up as an offshoot of Bradford MGC under the direction of a resourceful Indian woman, Rani Atma. She successfully recruited counsellors from the Muslim, Hindu and Sikh communities, and adapted the normal MGC training for them. Literature was produced in Hindi and Urdu. Clients were then able to state their problem and receive counselling in their own language. Other changes were also needed. It soon became apparent that, except when counselling took place cross-legged on the floor, more chairs were necessary. Marriage counselling offices normally have three chairs, one for the counsellor and two for the couple. Yet Asian women arrived for counselling with their sisters and cousins and aunts, all of whom expected to have their say about the problem.

Several clients telephoned but were too scared to leave home, and it felt right to visit them at home. Other clients described frustrating attempts to communicate with social workers or solicitors who, at that time in particular, were generally unable to provide a multi-lingual service. The counsellors' help extended well beyond the range of services traditionally provided in counselling agencies in Britain. At times they would accompany their clients to legal advisers or to court, acting as interpreters of language and of custom. The offices themselves had Asian decor and ornaments, which helped to make this the sort of place where Asians could feel at home.

After the first two years of the project, the offshoot body became independent as the Asian Family Counselling Service. Ostensibly this decision was taken for funding reasons. Central government had made available extra funds for minority ethnic projects. The director was well able to apply for her own grants and manage her own service. Nevertheless this decision concealed the underlying inability of the old established service and the new Asian one to work in partnership. The early hopes that joint training of counsellors would be introduced, that the old service might learn something from the more flexible ways of the new, that mobility between the two arms of the agency would develop, did not materialize. The Asians learnt from the mother body. The mother assimilated little or nothing from the daughter.

The Asian Family Counselling Service continues now to train and employ counsellors from various cultural communities, with its own independent management structure. It has two centres, in west London and Bradford, still under the direction of Rani Atma. She herself recently undertook a fellowship at the Tavistock Institute of Marital Studies, and carries out an extensive training programme.

The failure to integrate these two services highlights other aspects of racial issues in counselling, especially ignorance of, and unrecognized bias towards, other cultures. Cross-cultural counselling has traps for the unwary. The different scenarios involved in counselling between black counsellor and white client, white counsellor and black client, white counsellor and white client, and black counsellor and black client have been explored by Lago and Thompson (1991). Joyce Thompson played a major role in setting up the Association of Black Counsellors, and also a sub-committee of BAC on Racial Awareness in Counselling Education. She argued that all counselling agencies should examine their own practice and philosophy in relation to race. This examination may be sparked off by a lack of ethnic clients. Asking why this is so may lead to the realization of imbalance in their own staff composition. It should prompt recruitment of counsellors, trainers and committee members from other racial groups. The end product will be a leavening of different cultural understandings throughout the agency.

COUNSELLING BY TELEPHONE AND CORRESPONDENCE

The bulk of the counselling in all the above categories of agencies is carried out face to face. Most counsellors prefer to have direct personal contact with their clients, and find it more rewarding to work in depth with clients if they meet together on a regular basis. But this is not always possible. Many potential clients are too confused, apprehensive or ambivalent to ask for counselling. It is by no means only marital clients who show the sort of uncertainty which has been described by Brannen and Collard (1982: 232–3) as a 'help-seeking career'.

The agencies face a major challenge in how to encourage such people to 'knock on the door' or cross their threshold. Some of them help to make the bridge by offering to counsel on the telephone or through correspondence. The evidence of the letters received by the Advice Columnists of women's magazines is that there are thousands of women and men, young and old, who are concerned about personal problems and worried enough to write for advice. Many of these correspondents receive answers from these agony aunts encouraging them to contact a relevant agency.

Experience in the agencies I have been associated with shows that a remarkably small number of those so encouraged actually act on that advice. This may be because many of those correspondents were taking a tentative step in seeking help, just testing the water, so to speak, and were reassured to know that specialist help would be available if things deteriorated further. It may be because many of the correspondents did not want a face-to-face contact with an unknown counsellor, preferring to seek help from the safety of distance or only from a familiar figure in the media whose words they have learnt to value.

A third category is likely to include those who face practical impediments in knocking on a counselling door. Many of these are formidable – those housebound with children or elderly relatives; people immobile through disability; sufferers from agoraphobia; those living in remote and inaccessible districts; and those whose budgets do not stretch even as far as a bus fare to the counselling rooms.

Some of those who conceive of counselling as a long-term relationship are sceptical that the outcome of this sort of help may merely be transitory. Some of the older established agencies decline to engage in telephone counselling and restrict their correspondence to giving the address of the nearest counselling centre, in the belief that there is no substitute for face-to-face counselling. Counsellors who work by telephone or letter are not eligible for accreditation by the British Association of Counselling.

Nevertheless many people assert that they have been helped by telephone. This may be a once-only phone call. The British Association of Cancer United Patients (BACUP) counsels in person and by telephone. Many callers ring to get information and in so doing receive assurance. Ignorance may lie at the bottom of the fears and distress resulting from the illness. A half-hour's call with a sensitive and knowledgeable counsellor can bring relief and courage to face the future. Similarly, the counsellors of Childline do not know whom they are talking to, but by being there for children to make perhaps first disclosures about unhappy experiences, they may strengthen a child's wish to talk to a trusted relative or friendly teacher.

A single telephone call can prove a valuable catharsis. A young girl who felt stuck in her relationship with her boyfriend had many sleepless nights over whether to take the initiative to propose marriage to him. Her single-parent mother knew of her uncertainty but, mindful of her own experience, took the line that 'it's up to you'. In a long telephone call to a Youth Counselling helpline the girl poured out all her frustration, all the possible alternatives. The counsellor was scarcely able to get a word in. The rush of words released pent-up emotion and freed her of her uncertainty. She thanked the counsellor for her advice ('What advice?', thought the counsellor). She did not need to accept the invitation to ring back in a week or two. Within six months she and her boyfriend were married.

Not all telephone calls are like this. Some callers ring back. Times can be fixed in advance so that the client can know that the same counsellor will be on duty. The same applies to correspondence. One reply with some relevant information or a booklist may suffice for some of those who write. Others keep up a correspondence over months or years. Bereaved people find particular comfort in writing down their thoughts and feelings, and some bereavement agencies encourage this.

A letter from one widower started as follows:

My doctor told me to write to you. I just feel so down and helpless. After my first wife died, I managed to pick myself up again and three years later I married a dear friend of hers. It was like a wonderful new beginning. Now she's been killed in a terrible car crash. All my happiness has been pulled from underneath me. It's so cruel.

The counsellor replied sympathetically, in effect saying 'Write again and tell me all about it'. A long reply came by return, giving many details of both marriages, ending with the words 'It's such a load off my mind to write about all this'. Two more letters came in quick succession. Then there was a gap of one month, with a letter saying he had got back to work but none of his mates knew how to talk about his loss, so there was an awkward silence hanging over everything. He wrote in the middle of the night when he had woken feeling deeply depressed.

Subsequent letters were more spread out. They came when some event or date prompted an acute spasm of grief – his wife's birthday, the anniversary of the crash, the laying of her tombstone. The correspondents never met. Only ten letters were exchanged, yet the widower punctuated his with phrases like 'It's as if I've known you all my life' and 'You understand what I'm going through so well that I feel I can tell you anything'.

The last letter was three years on:

The third anniversary hit me unexpectedly. I'd thought I'd got over her death, but I kept dissolving into tears for no reason for about a week. It's silly really because I've just become secretary of the Bowls Club and there's more than enough to do. The tears just made me realise what a wonderful support you've been over all this time.

SEEKING HELP

In most of the independent agencies clients refer themselves. They may come on the recommendation of a third party, a social worker, perhaps, or a medical practitioner, but the relationship is a private one between client and agency. The agency is free to accept the client or not, though extraneous factors may play a part in that. For instance, in many parts of Britain there have been waiting lists for counselling, and this can act as a deterrent to would-be clients. On the clients' side there may be considerable ambivalence about seeking help, or they may have made a series of attempts which somehow have been doomed to failure. In their study of marital clients, as already mentioned, Brannen and Collard (1982) describe many as having a 'help-seeking career' in which several stages are identified: first, awareness of a problem; second, defining it as a marital problem; third, deciding to get help. For many this involves approaching a GP, or visiting a Citizens' Advice Bureau, Family Planning Clinic or similar agency. It is often only after several steps that they refer themselves to a marital agency (Brannen and Collard 1982: 82–3).

The path to help is by no means a simple one, and may depend on fortuitous circumstances. For instance, the study quoted above showed that helpful referrals often came from a locum or a new GP who sees from a different perspective the symptoms which had been treated previously purely medically by the regular doctors. The moral must be that it is often worth getting a second opinion!

Clients reach counselling by many different routes and with varying degrees of understanding about what to expect. Counsellors anticipate uncertainty or ambivalence in their first contact with new clients. To help clarify expectations on both sides, counselling often starts with exploring with the individual client what steps he has had to take to get him as far as the counselling room.

However, counselling is now more widely understood. The atmosphere has changed dramatically since the 1970s when the debate was about whether counselling was relevant or not. Many of the people who came in the early days for counselling came rather furtively, driven by a sense of shame and guilt. It was common for clients to start by saying 'Don't tell my parents I've come to see you' or 'My family would be horrified if they knew I'd come here'. Many marital clients came without the knowledge of their spouses. The agencies themselves favoured being situated in anonymous premises with small discreet notices on the door, so as not to embarrass the clients who came to them. The whole atmosphere was one of secrecy.

In less than 20 years a major change in attitudes to help-seeking has been witnessed. We are used now to much more openness about personal problems. There is nothing unusual about references to abortion or HIV/AIDS and the need for 'safe sex' in the press. Individuals speaking on television and radio air their intimate feelings or describe their emotional and relationship difficulties freely. Problem pages in magazines abound. In earlier years marital clients customarily were loath to introduce the subject of sex. They would talk about anything else first. It might well be not until the third interview that one of them would say sheepishly, 'And, by the way, things are not too good in bed.' Today's clients' opening remarks are more likely to be 'Our problem is premature ejaculation' or 'He can't keep it up long enough to get it in'!

In no way does this mean that people bear their problems lightly. There can still be great anguish, a deep sense of failure and despair, and often surprising ignorance. But the sense of isolation has lessened. There is more knowledge about how and where to turn for help, more 'doors to knock on'. And there is a more conducive climate for asking for help. To do so now is considered a sensible thing to do rather than a foolish or risky one.

This changed expectation has put pressure on all counselling agencies to provide a more competent and more specialist service. Voluntary organizations are not exempt from this. As soon as agencies offer a counselling service, the public expects them to have authority and be competent, and professional workers see them as a source of referral. Management committees in the voluntary sector are increasingly uncomfortable about shielding behind the excuse that they are 'only voluntary' organizations. Nor are the volunteers who work in such agencies prepared to accept mediocrity. The next chapter examines some of the requirements for the counselling agencies seeking to meet these demands.

THREE

The practice of counselling in the voluntary sector

AMATEUR OR PROFESSIONAL?

' "When *I* use a word," Humpty Dumpty said, in a rather scornful tone, "it means just what I choose it to mean – neither more nor less." ' The voluntary sector takes much the same approach in describing its work, so enquirers into the Looking Glass world of counselling, like Alice, can be excused for being perplexed at what is on offer.

Some of the organizations are clear that their helpers are called 'counsellors', that they provide counselling for people called 'clients', and that their counsellors receive supervision from professional supervisors. Their uncertainty may lie in the boundary between counselling and psychotherapy, and how far their counsellors are becoming involved in therapeutic relationships which may not be appropriate for that particular agency.

Other agencies provide personal help based on counselling insights and call their volunteers by such terms as 'befrienders', 'listeners', 'visitors' or 'workers'. They stress that their helpers have not received sufficient training to be classified as counsellors, and that counselling implies too formal a relationship between the helpers and the helped in their field. Timms and Blampiad (1980) explored all these possibilities in their search for the most apposite description of the workers in the Catholic Marriage Advisory Council. They settled for 'formal friend'.

Similar ambiguities exist as to what to call those who are helped. The term 'patient' tends to be avoided, except in organizations which are closely linked to the medical services. In more current vogue are words such as 'caller', 'user' or 'customer' which satisfactorily convey the sense of autonomy and choice for the recipient, but which some think imply too much of a commercial relationship. The term 'client' is more commonly applied, but again some agencies do not use it because they feel it to be too formal and undermining of the spontaneity which is the particular strength of the voluntary sector. Other organizations use a descriptive title for those they help – disabled person, victim or bereaved person.

Terms also differ in describing the person who supports the helper. This may depend on the genesis of the organization. The most usual term in social work practice is 'supervisor', but in a medical environment that word carries negative managerial overtones. Imported from the world of education is the function of 'tutor'. Some agencies opt for the term 'consultant', which may imply a shared relationship, with the onus on the worker to seek consultation rather than on the consultant to impose it. Those favouring less formal nomenclature often use 'support' as a way of describing the process, and 'supporter' or 'support person' for the one who provides it.

At one level this might be thought to be merely a matter of semantics, and the last word would be left with Humpty Dumpty. But there are serious issues underlying these questions, such as the nature of the helping process and the degree of authority exercised by the agency and its helpers. Befrienders may feel themselves to be just friends. The essence of friendship, however, is mutuality. Befrienders who are selected and officially appointed by agencies work on behalf of their agency and carry responsibility for it. This inevitably puts them in an unequal relationship with the person who has sought help.

Similarly, visitors may see themselves as friends or supporters, but they bring with them the promise of their agencies to try to assist. Their effectiveness may lie in 'being there' rather than in the conscious exercise of counselling skills, and they may not fully appreciate the value of their personal contribution; but their actions stem from the corporate wisdom and experience of their organizations. Likewise, those who support the helpers may be apprehensive about what is expected of them as supervisors and describe their role as just giving support. But essential to this process is the element of authority vested in them by their agency for their task of nurturing the counsellors, and giving or withholding approval of their counselling.

To some extent these differences may represent the masculine and feminine conceptions of giving help. The feminine tends to focus on the process, and to emphasize spontaneity, warmth and immediacy. The masculine tends to place more stress on boundaries, roles and structures. If so, it is scarcely surprising that the voluntary sector, where women far outnumber men, sometimes places low priority on role, nomenclature and authority. Yet in so far as counselling is, or seems to be, a nebulous activity, definitions of role can help to clarify its purpose and meaning. It may not matter whether the client grasps the full significance of such definitions, but it is important for counsellors and supervisors to be clear in their own minds about what they are aiming to do.

The importance of accurate definitions is well illustrated in bereavement organizations. A counsellor goes to the home of a bereaved person in response to a telephone call. The client is likely to be in grief and confusion and unclear about what he needs. The appointments secretary has not been able to convey more than that someone from the branch will visit. It is all too easy from that unspecific beginning for a relationship to develop in which the natural course of events is for the client to talk through his grief and for the bereavement visitor to listen. She may never get an opportunity to explain that she is there as a counsellor with the objective of helping the client to navigate his river of grief until such time as he can manage it on his own. In the intensity and immediacy of the grief, objectives are easily lost by counsellor and client. Counsellors often have great difficulty knowing when and how to bring this sort of counselling to a conclusion. The client can go on seeing the counsellor as a regular visitor. The counsellor then feels herself slipping out of role. Part of the trouble is that the roles and process have not been made clear at any time during the counselling relationship. Recognizing early on that they were client and counsellor might have helped them to hold in mind the whole point of the contact between them.

On training courses with new counsellors these issues frequently dominate discussions. As they wrestle with the appropriate terminology, it is apparent that they are struggling to come to terms with becoming a formal helper. Many have had long experience of helping informally as neighbour, colleague or friend. The terms 'counsellor' and 'client' confront them with the significance of moving from the informality of friendship to the formality of the helping relationship. Their skill and intuition may not change, but they have to become accustomed to the additional authority they bear as workers in their organizations.

Similarly, the people they help are known as and indeed see themselves as clients. In so defining themselves they have taken a step in acknowledging their need for help. It is often said that asking for help is the beginning of the healing process. Someone who is troubled with problems and continually demands the time and attention of friends may be using these friendships to avoid taking action to deal with the problems. Self-referral to a counselling agency can then represent a significant move forward in accepting the need for personal change.

To benefit from counselling, clients need the motivation to change. An important aspect of the intake procedure in some agencies is assessing whether applicants are sufficiently strongly and realistically motivated. In situations where there is external pressure to receive counselling the motivation may be particularly questionable. Counsellors taking referrals in doctors' surgeries have to assess with care whether the patients wish to become their clients. In penal settings it is even more difficult. As a young probation officer, I had under supervision a wealthy City broker, old enough to be my father, who had been arrested for soliciting. With whisky decanter ever at the ready, he turned every visit of mine into a social occasion. Though nominally my client, he successfully evaded the commitment to change which the court had envisaged for him.

In other subtle ways some of the people who come under the aegis of voluntary organizations are reluctant about becoming clients. Some are referred by a third party, such as a medical auxiliary or neighbour, and may have only a hazy idea of what they are agreeing to. Some come at the instigation of a relative and are only going through the motions of seeking help to please the family. For others, the first approach has been made by the agency, and they do not feel able to decline the offer of help. People in such categories need to be faced with whether or not they are prepared to commit themselves to become clients in more than name only.

Precise definitions and roles will doubtless continue to vary between agencies. In exploring the common issues here I use the terms 'client', 'counsellor' and 'supervisor' throughout, because I believe that they clarify the relative positions and commitment of the different participants in the helping triangle.

THE SETTING

One of the fundamentals of counselling is to create a 'safe place' for clients to be able to express their thoughts and feelings. Clients are liable to feel anything but safe – more likely confused, traumatized, chaotic, rejected or suspicious. They need to feel that they can talk about these feelings, can admit to them and explore them with some hope of alleviation or relief.

The relationship offered by the counsellor is the main factor in creating a sense of safety. Marital clients in Hunt's (1985: 69) research spoke of how important it was for them that counsellors offered hope, support, encouragement and permission to behave differently. But the setting is also important in creating a confidential atmosphere. The anxiety level of one of Hunt's couples was increased by poor soundproofing. The husband commented: 'It didn't seem from what we heard from the other rooms as if they were having a very high success rate. Have you any figures as to how many marriages you save?' (Hunt 1985: 57).

Several other clients commented on the uncertainty they had felt about the amount of time available for their sessions. Just as they thought they had reached a haven where they were being accepted and listened to, it seemed to them that the counsellor called time, and they were suddenly exposed and vulnerable again. One client who came with his wife recollected that 'the session lasted 50 to 55 minutes so we both had to leave in the middle of a row. The counsellor didn't say how long we had and time flies' (Hunt 1985: 58).

Hunt concludes that an essential element of creating a sense of security is indicating clearly the aim of the session and how much time is available. A reminder later in the session that there is about ten minutes left for rounding off, counters the risk of leaving clients up in the air. How to end sessions in ways which leave clients not too emotionally disturbed is a crucial subject to include in the training and preparation of counsellors.

The physical setting has an important part to play. The example above illustrates the need for soundproofing. To help clients relax and feel able to talk freely, it is also essential to provide privacy and reasonable comfort. Such requirements pose a problem for many agencies in the voluntary sector. Many a time in visiting voluntary organizations I have climbed many stairs with no lifts for the elderly or disabled, have shivered in cold waiting rooms, sat on rickety chairs and felt depressed by the echoing corridors and shabby decorations. For many clients the warmth of the counsellors overcomes these environmental deficiencies. But others doubtless feel their own sense of worthlessness confirmed by the 'worthless' setting in which they are received, or become even more depressed by the surroundings.

I am not suggesting that anyone is happy with these conditions. The stark reality in the voluntary sector is that a large percentage of the expenditure goes on accommodation. Suitable rooms, accesssible to the client population, constantly strain the budget. Underfunded voluntary agencies often have to resort to taking short-term leases on inner-city offices due for demolition, or have to make do with uncomfortable and gloomy premises in run-down churches, damp terraced houses in slum areas and other undesirable locations. Many management committees find their agenda dominated by the problem of finding satisfactory counselling offices. They are forced to conclude, reluctantly, that substandard accommodation is preferable to the drastic alternative of closing down the service.

Much care and effort goes into making the best of poor premises. House committees or groups of Friends do wonders with pictures, second-hand furniture and flowers. Help with decorating or gardening is given by volunteers or groups from Intermediate Treatment schemes. Apparently small items can loom large in a client's impression. And a box of tissues within reach implies that it is all right to get upset.

Sometimes the best efforts to strike a right balance between a domestic atmosphere and a place where business can be done is ruined by matters which concern the agency but can be an affront to the client. Two posters come to mind. One dominating the pleasing decor of a youth counselling room asked: 'Do YOU need an AIDS/HIV positive test?' The other was a prominent notice on the wall in an adult counselling agency which reminded clients: 'Each counselling session costs us £15.25. We hope you will discuss with your counsellor how much you can contribute towards that.' Each poster certainly reflected reality, but also undermined the accepting, welcoming atmosphere that the counsellors were trying to create.

The issue of smoking has become a controversial one, which requires sensitivity on all sides. Agencies have to balance the wishes of non-smokers among their workers and clients against the strong need felt by some clients to smoke during counselling. It is not uncommon for clients to reach for a cigarette when they are struggling to express particularly stressful feelings. My personal reaction is to encourage them to smoke at such times, and I like to have an ashtray ready to pass to them. As counsellors we are helping clients to face their stress openly and I do not like to deprive them then of their accustomed means of comfort. However, this practice is increasingly unacceptable to colleagues. More and more agencies are following the trend of either creating smoke-free rooms or having a strict no-smoking policy.

HOME VISITS

Some organizations argue strongly that all counselling should take place in rooms provided by the agency. In this way a neutral atmosphere is provided, where clients are removed from all external distractions. The clients' commitment to the possibility of change through counselling is tested since they have to make the effort to get to the office. Home visits are seen as time-consuming and costly since the counsellors do all the travelling and the agency meets the travel expenses. More significantly, it is held that home visits are also likely to divert counsellors from the task of counselling since the client as host is able to arrange the setting, leaving the counsellor with little control over the external constraints of telephone, visitors or family.

A few organizations undertake most of their counselling through home visits, especially disability and bereavement groups and victim support. Given the chance, many clients opt for a home visit. In their follow-up interviews both Hunt (1985) and Brannen and Collard (1982) were struck by their respondents' preferences for home interviews. Two-thirds of Hunt's (1985: 10) sample elected to be interviewed at home. Brannen and Collard (1982: 219) observed that their research interviews were welcome as they provided 'some of the safeguards and confidentiality of the agency . . . a degree of power for respondents which was more akin to relationships with confidants . . . and respondents were interviewed in their own homes.'

The arguments for home visits are fourfold. First, counsellors literally enter into the world of their clients. This may be especially important in grief work.

> Entry of this kind is a powerful gesture on the part of the counsellor. Not only the bereaved person, but also the counsellor, are made forcibly aware of the empty space which now fills the home. The attention of the bereaved person is focussed upon the reality of their loss and also their consequent appeal for help.
>
> (Hockey 1990: 53)

Some counsellors also feel they gain a more accurate understanding of clients and their practical difficulties if they talk with them in their own setting. They see for themselves the practical hazards which create isolation for the physically handicapped, the drawers of business correspondence which leave the bereaved overwhelmed and helpless, the vulnerable windows which anchor victims of burglary in their houses. Counselling can focus so intently on the inner world of the clients that the significance of the practical difficulties which they face can be underestimated, as the research mentioned in Chapter 2 reported (Mayer and Timms 1970).

Second, things which can be seen as intrusive in one-to-one counselling sessions may in fact offer help to the counsellor who can be flexible enough to use them. Family photographs, treasured possessions in the house or a garden with special memories may open up opportunities to talk about sensitive matters. Children or other family members can be helped to share their part in the trauma of a break-in or death. These intrusions may or may not have the potential for assisting in the process of counselling. Good counsellors find ways of dealing with the unexpected.

In one instance, over some weeks, a counsellor visited a woman whose daughter had died. Her 16-year-old son showed great ambivalence about joining in. He hovered awkwardly, neither staying nor going away. After several visits he took the counsellor to his room and took out of his cupboard his mementos and photographs of his sister. He said he could not display them for fear of upsetting his parents. His mother stayed downstairs while the boy poured out his frustration and grief at not being able to talk to his parents about the death. This proved a catalyst. Two visits later the counsellor, the boy and the parents were able to look together at the souvenirs and talk about what they meant to them all.

The third reason for home visits is that there are many people in vulnerable conditions who cannot bring themselves to venture out to an unknown office. They may be frail, elderly or physically handicapped. They may be fit physically but so traumatized that the only place where they feel safe enough to trust themselves with anyone is their own home. No counsellor should visit anyone at home without realizing this frailty and appreciating both the privilege and precariousness of crossing the threshold into someone else's house.

Finally, even with agencies that prefer counselling to take place outside the home, geographical realities have to be considered. A local agency which aims to provide a service throughout a large rural county may find its counsellors and clients widely dispersed. With such distances the prime consideration in allocating cases may be who lives nearest to whom. Both may be far from any counselling rooms. Sometimes it is possible to find a neutral meeting place, accessible to client and counsellor, such as a doctor's surgery, health centre or village hall. But at times common sense can point to meeting in the home of either the client or the counsellor. Most agencies are not keen for counsellors to see clients on a regular basis in their own homes, particularly if nothing is previously known about the client. Safeguards are laid down. However, in a few cases, after checking out the situation with a supervisor, geographical imperatives point to the use of the counsellor's house.

CONFIDENTIALITY

One of the features that distinguishes counsellors who work in an organization such as a voluntary agency from those who work privately is that the clients are the clients of the agency. They are not the clients of the individual counsellor. This is easily overlooked since the relationship between counsellor and client is such an intimate and personal one. The main healing medium is their personal interaction, so both parties are naturally very significant to each other.

In this close relationship, dependency and possessiveness can develop. Serge Blackie describes the strong pull she felt with one client.

> During this time I grew very fond of Carol, breaking all my previously perceived rules about not becoming emotionally involved with clients. I identified with much of her childhood experience and felt angry for both of us and protective of her. My early training had emphasised the importance of keeping my feelings out of the counselling relationship, so that is what I struggled to do. The effect of this, though, was to create an artificial distance between us which was uncomfortable for me . . . I came down from my pedestal and left my 'perfect-counsellor' role behind me.
>
> (Mearns and Dryden 1990: 119)

With such strong feelings of attachment, it is small wonder that a culture of 'my client' and 'my counsellor' abounds. It can become difficult for the agency to know what is happening in the counselling room in its name, or to decide how and when to call its counsellors to account. On the whole this task is left to supervisors, who discuss with their counsellors issues of continuing or ending counselling. However, supervisors and counsellors are both likely to be influenced by the same technical considerations. The organizer may know of other considerations, such as the pressure of the waiting list or the existence of emergency cases. It is important that agencies establish a mechanism in which all such factors are weighed against each other, so that decisions about priorities are not impeded either by possessiveness by counsellors or by inappropriate claims to confidentiality.

Each agency should have clear rules about confidentiality within which its counsellors work. Many of their guidelines are based on the model Code of Ethics and Practice first produced by the British Association of Counselling in 1984 and since updated. Others have produced their own rules. For instance, Cruse Bereavement Care has produced a document called *Confidentiality: Principle and Practice for Cruse Branches* (Cruse 1988) which runs to eight pages. It covers such issues as good practice; exemptions to confidentiality; case records; information in the office; and imparting information to other agencies, family members, professional advisers, research workers and the media. It strongly emphasizes the need for all workers to be sensitive with any personal information about clients or enquirers. It gives guidance as to which matters are confidential to counsellors and their supervisors, which matters it is appropriate to share with branch officers, and what information should be on branch files.

Conscious that their counsellors are drawn from the local community and may be known by or mix with clients and potential clients in shops, schools or churches, voluntary agencies fiercely guard their confidentiality. Gossiping with confidential information is the greatest offence of all. With a constant flow through the office of clients, counsellors and other workers, there needs to be a firm discipline imposed about all client information.

Some agencies allow a few instances where confidentiality may be breached. This may only occur officially with the consent of an authorized officer, and preferably with the client's knowledge. Such exemptions are only likely where a counsellor has been given information about child abuse; where there are police enquiries into serious crimes of violence; or when a counsellor is concerned that a threat of suicide may be carried out. Not all agencies have a common mind about this. Some maintain that confidentiality should never be broken.

Counsellor and agency must ponder all factors carefully before taking action to alert the appropriate authority. They know how important it is to distinguish between fact and fantasy in a client's story. This line can be especially blurred with clients talking about their experience of sexual abuse in the family. Similarly, publicity about a sensational case in the media may give rise to fears and fantasies in clients' minds. At the time when the Yorkshire Ripper was being hunted, marrriage counsellors heard many a woman confide that her husband was he. Clients' allegations must be treated seriously but with caution.

Voluntary agencies are engaged in a delicate balancing act. Their workers have not relinquished their normal duties as citizens to report crime. Counsellors cannot be accessories to it. Yet voluntary agencies are a proper place of sanctuary to which troubled people may feel able to turn because of the agencies' freedom from statutory obligations. Ideally in the privacy of the counselling room their fears and experiences may be openly explored and an outcome satisfactory to both parties can be achieved. It should be a rule of all voluntary organizations that, in any borderline case, counsellors keep a supervisor or authorized person informed of the issue. This is important for the counsellors' own peace of mind and support, as well as for the integrity of the agency.

On one occasion an experienced counsellor shared with her supervisor her dilemma at hearing of a possible instance of abuse of a young person. In the course of counselling a client had said that her 12-year-old daughter had told her of an approach made to her by her new stepfather. As a result the mother and stepfather were invited to come together and the incident was openly discussed with the counsellor. The latter felt that the mother–daughter relationship was a positive one which the mother was handling very responsibly. The couple continued in regular counselling and used the occasion to explore various aspects of their first marriages which had previously been taboo, as well as their present family relationships. The supervisor was faced with the dilemma of whether to report the matter to the statutory authorities, or whether to encourage the counsellor to continue to work with the couple, and also possibly to see mother and daughter together. Disclosure would result in action by police and social services, and the outcome was unpredictable. In consultation with her colleagues the supervisor was satisfied that the family was receiving the best possible help and decided not to disclose the matter; but she continued to monitor the case closely.

There are occasions on which counsellors are liable to receive a subpoena from a court to attend to give evidence concerning something said in the privacy of the counselling room. Counsellors have never been accorded 'privilege', that is, absolute exemption from having to disclose confidential information given to them. The threat of subpoena for marriage counsellors was not uncommon in civil actions when divorce was determined by proof of matrimonial fault, although now it is rare. On such occasions counsellors must obey the dictates of their own conscience, but it behoves their agency to provide them with legal advice and support, and, if necessary, legal representation in court to guide them about what questions they are required to answer.

CLIENT RECORDS

The issue of confidentiality applies directly to the keeping of written information about clients. Security of information is vital. Most counselling offices are visited by all sorts of people, and personal information which is identifiable must be rigorously safeguarded. A good rule is to keep the minimum possible. Lockable filing cabinets are essential. Personal records should be kept no longer than necessary. Most agencies set a time limit beyond which all records are destroyed. Some set this at two years, others at five.

What sort of records to keep requires careful consideration. One complication is that client records are kept for several different purposes. Another is that the facilities for maintaining a confidential filing system vary markedly between agencies. It has proved impossible to find one system which meets every need.

Agencies need to keep notes of some kind about each client, be it on computer, card index or in a day book. It may be just 'male rang at 2.15 a.m., no name given.' In a face-to-face counselling agency it is more likely to include name, address and telephone number, date and reason for application, perhaps information about the family. To this will be added the action taken by the person on duty. This information is basically for administrative use in the centre. It also ensures continuity if clients ring again. In some agencies this is all that is required by way of notes.

Other organizations have reason to want more information. They wish to carry out market research. They wish to know what sections of the community they are neglecting, so they are interested in the age of clients, their socio-economic group, their ethnic group, employment status, length of disability or marriage, and so on. Some agencies are required to monitor their clientele in accordance with equal opportunities legislation.

A further need is to enable agencies to produce a comprehensive profile of their services in order to inform the public, educate their local authorities and convince potential contributors of funds. The latter are interested in what sorts of problem clients present with, where they have been referred from, what other places they have already been to for help, how many are married, divorced, gay,

living alone, and so on. It is tempting to produce a lengthy questionnaire for each new enquirer to fill in; this may serve the common good but does nothing to help the individual client.

Counsellors have particularly in mind the interests of their clients. Some agencies believe that any note-keeping comes between
counsellor and client, creating a barrier, so to speak, in the relationship. Their counsellors tend to do no more than jot down the dates
of their encounters. Some of these agencies work from the private
houses of their secretaries or organizers so have no central office
with secure filing cabinets. They are naturally wary of confidential
information being held in counsellors' houses.

Most counsellors take the view that they need to take some notes,
in order to remember the names or ages of significant people or
events in the client's lives, to remind them of salient points and to
note issues to follow up subsequently. Some counsellors write as
much as they can of each interview, as a way of reflecting on it and
preparing themselves for the next one. These notes also serve as
milestones to look back on to see what progress has been made
during counselling. Counsellors argue that these notes help them to
help clients more effectively.

There has been a fundamental change in thinking about client
records in recent years. All notes used to be kept by counsellors and
were not disclosed to clients. The basic principle now is that clients
have a right to see anything written about them. This practice is enshrined in the Data Protection Act of 1991 by which all agencies
keeping records on a word-processor with a database are required
to be registered. Clients should be told at an early stage that counsellors make their own private notes, and that these are available
for clients to see if they wish. In practice, clients rarely ask to see
them. Some counsellors choose to make record-keeping a collaborative matter. Counsellor and client agree at the end of each session
what they wish to record about it. This practice is time-consuming,
however, and may detract from the immediacy of the session.

Case records are used for two other purposes. One is for supervision and/or assessment of the counsellor. In agencies such as
Relate supervisors require counsellors to prepare for supervision by
producing full case notes. The accreditation processes in BAC and
other accrediting systems rely partly on examination of case records.
These case notes do not carry name or identifying details, and counsellors have to bear in mind that clients may exercise their right to
know what is being said and written about them, and to whom.

Whatever case notes are written, it is important that they do
not identify the person concerned. Security cannot be guaranteed.

Several counselling offices have been broken into and filing cabinets forced open. It is good practice to keep names and addresses in one place and continuation sheets in another, with only a code number as a cross reference. In that way confidentiality concerning an identifiable person is unlikely to be breached.

Research workers have a professional interest in the information in agency files. It is obviously of interest to the social historian to learn what are identified as problems for which help is sought in a rapidly changing world, and to chart the changes in the type of help provided. However, experience shows that attempts to graft a research project on to an already existing system of documentation come to nought. It is true that there is a mine of sociological data in counselling filing cabinets, but such data have been acquired with therapeutic ends in mind and do not adapt for research purposes.

Any research project realistically has to start from scratch. The significant questions have to be framed. A pilot has to be run. Then, if at all possible, a small sample should be tested rather than the whole of the agency's clientele. Evaluation projects involve administrators and counsellors in time-consuming activity and cost. The results are often difficult to collate, so the end product can prove of little use. The outcome may have long-term effects, but that may seem of little value to hard-pressed organizing secretaries, often working from their homes. Any large-scale study needs to be planned with an accurate awareness of the demands that will be made on administrative resources.

PROMOTING THE AGENCY

Although some agencies, such as Victim Support and Compassionate Friends, make a first approach by phone or letter to people who are eligible as clients, most agencies expect clients to make the first approach. Agencies need to make themselves known locally to the public. Posters or cards can be displayed in clinics, churches, display boards and surgeries. Many Councils of Voluntary Service produce lists of available helping agencies in their areas. National directories are published by umbrella organizations such as BAC (1991) and the National Association of Bereavement Services (1992). These give addresses of services available throughout Britain, without conferring a seal of approval.

Local agencies also need to ensure that accurate information about them is available to the other organizations in the area. Not only should it be known what services they provide, but it is also vital to publish details such as times of opening. Unless they are clearly stated, it is only too easy to acquire a reputation locally for never being available. Without regular communication among them, agencies rely on second-hand information. Much may depend on the quality of relationships among the staff of the different agencies. If they are not good, agencies may be unduly influenced by reports by new clients of unsatisfactory experiences in other organizations. Referral of clients between agencies is a complex matter and will be considered in more detail in Chapter 5.

It is essential to produce simple explanatory pamphlets and make them available to the public. One from the Wantage Counselling Service explains:

> Most of us experience times in our life when we feel under pressure and find it hard to cope. Sometimes we need the support and understanding of someone who can offer another perspective, helping us to fresh insight and a clearer view. Counselling offers time to explore the situation, a sustaining relationship, trust and confidentiality. Working with a trained counsellor in a safe setting, it is possible to try out new ways of being, to gain greater understanding of oneself and the freedom to choose and act in more satisfying ways. The capacity to cope can be regained together with the appreciation that life can be different.

The pamphlet goes on to state when counselling is available and how to make contact.

Good publicity is much more difficult to achieve than might be apparent. Keeping an accurate and active profile in a catchment area takes time and costs money. It is always helpful to put pamphlets about the organization in libraries, clinics and CABx. Supplies have to be continually renewed, so print runs are necessarily large. Notices quickly get dog-eared and give an unwelcoming impression. Even information such as times of availability or contact telephone numbers become outdated, especially with small organizations working from people's homes. A publicity officer with flair and enthusiasm is an essential requirement for all voluntary organizations.

The media are a valuable resource. The local press and radio are hungry for any kind of local news. Features based on human interest stories, with care taken to safeguard the confidentiality of actual clients, remind the community of the agency's existence. Many potential clients, and indeed potential counsellors, have to see or

hear the message several times before they make the link with
themselves. One client told an intake worker:

> I've known about you for ages, since we did a project at
> school. Then a couple of months ago I saw a notice in my GP's
> surgery and I realized there was a branch in the town. Then
> last week I heard one of your counsellors on local radio and
> she made it sound like a personal invitation. So here I am.

The traditional high publicity spot for many agencies is the annual general meeting. This is a legal requirement for all charities.
It tends to be used as the annual open window, with all goods on
display. There are formalities to get through – elections to committees, presentation of financial accounts, appointment of auditors,
and an account, often printed, of the year's work. This business is
sometimes completed in ten minutes, but may well take over an
hour. The art is in giving an informative account of triumphs and
problems. On occasions this is skilfully done, with various members
talking about their side of the work, and proves an informative
event. A more frequent practice is to tack a speaker on to the end
of the business, hoping this will attract people from the community
to attend.

The formula works sometimes. However, an undue proportion of
time and effort can go into making preparations for it, often with
disappointing results. It may fail to address the different expectations in the audience. There are likely to be members of the public
present, including representatives of local authorities, interested
in basic facts about the work. People from colleague organizations
and the professions may want to explore how to work together.
The workers in the organization itself may need fresh inspiration
or challenge. It is difficult to satisfy these disparate needs and
expectations.

It is worth experimenting with more innovative ways of meeting these needs. The first thing to abandon is perhaps the time-
honoured all-purpose evening AGM which is a survival from
pre-television days and often poorly attended. Lunchtime or late
afternoon meetings on relevant subjects targeted at specific groups
can prove a more effective use of time and effort. Open meetings
with good public speakers can be arranged, if desired, without the
encumbrance of what frequently turns out to be boring and badly
conducted business. The AGM must still be advertised and open to
the public, but it can be a low-key meeting, aimed at the committed,
who can be thanked for their work over the past year and involved in
planning for the future.

THE REMIT OF THE AGENCY

Counselling agencies in the voluntary sector divide into those which are generic and those which specialize. The generic services include most of the youth counselling services and those associated with the Westminster Pastoral Foundation. As the pamphlet from Wantage quoted above illustrates, they talk in terms such as offering 'support and understanding' and 'trying out new ways of being'. Problems and symptoms tend to be avoided, though some mention help for people who are depressed. Some emphasize positive features such as emotional growth, re-evaluating lifestyles and personal development.

These agencies present a contrast to the problem-centred networks which have been the main consideration of this book so far. These specialist organizations make clear what is the focus of their counselling, generally by their titles – Alcohol Concern; Release (for the welfare of people using drugs); SPOD (Association to Aid the Sexual and Personal Relationships of People with a Disability); and BACUP (British Association of Cancer United Patients). The agencies may have a clear conception of the boundaries of their remit, what are valid issues for their counsellors to be working on and which ones lie outside their specialist concerns.

For the counsellor, however, this borderline may not be so clear. The presenting problem which the client brings may be the tip of an iceberg. Discussing how to cut down heavy drinking is likely to lead to exploring what has been the cause of it and may uncover deep but suppressed feelings such as guilt about sexual identity. Seeking guidance in mid-career may entail weighing up the conflicting demands of job, home and leisure interests (Rapoport 1970: 232–4), and trying to ameliorate difficulties in family or personal relationships. A client's grief over the death of a father may face the bereavement counsellor with the dilemma of how deeply to explore the client's long-felt but unresolved personal inadequacies.

Counselling training underlines the importance of seeing individuals as whole people. Most presenting symptoms cannot just be isolated and cured without reference to other aspects of the client's life. This presents counsellors in specialist agencies with dilemmas. They must be alert as to when they are overstepping the boundary of the agency's remit and should encourage clients to seek more appropriate help elsewhere.

The need to keep a focus can be seen in grief counselling. Worden (1991: 10–18) has identified four tasks of mourning which counselling can facilitate: accepting the reality of the loss; working through to the pain of grief; adjusting to an environment in which the deceased is no longer present; and emotionally relocating the deceased and moving on in life. Counsellors may be of use in any or all of these tasks. They enable clients to express their desolation and anger, give voice to their inner questions or work at making sense of their loss. They may help them make decisions about the present or plans for the future. These are all valid tasks. But counsellors need to recognize when they are being drawn into aspects of life which are not related to the grief. Then they must either find another source of help or bring the counselling to an end in a way which does not leave the client feeling rejected.

In the training of bereavement counsellors, a person's grief can be likened to a river. Both have a starting point and an end. Some rivers come to a sudden end at the sea; others flow out into an estuary and, as with some grief, it is not clear when the full course has been run. Grief often flows slowly, meandering for long stretches, seemingly getting nowhere. At other times it is in spate, threatening to overflow the banks and get out of control. The counsellor acts as the bank, holding the river in its passage to the sea. There are many temptations to divert up tributaries concerned with other aspects of life. The client may wish the counsellor to help to solve all life's problems. The counsellor has to resist the temptation to collude with that wish, and keep the focus on enabling the river of grief to flow. Recognizing that there is a tributary calling for additional specialist attention, and identifying where that help can be found, is a vital skill to acquire.

Counsellors in all settings must guard against being drawn into issues which are outside the competence of their agencies. In a voluntary agency they are able to seek advice from colleagues about when and how to resist taking up inappropriate matters raised by clients. Such help and advice are best provided in supervision.

SUPERVISION

An essential aspect of counselling is that the counsellor receives regular supervision. BAC (1984: Section 3.3) states unequivocally: 'Counsellors monitor their counselling work through regular supervision by professionally competent supervisors and are able to account to clients and colleagues for what they do and why.' If this requirement is necessary for counsellors who have received a lengthy professional training it is clearly desirable in the more *ad hoc* world of the voluntary sector.

Supervision is provided in different ways. Most commonly, in voluntary organizations small groups of counsellors meet regularly (say, fortnightly or monthly) with a supervisor. This gives opportunities for talking about matters of concern to individuals or the group, examining difficult counselling cases, increasing skill and providing mutual support. If the group grows too large for engendering a sense of trust, which can happen when there are more than ten or twelve members, it is best to divide into two groups.

Alternatively, or preferably additionally, supervision is given on a one-to-one basis. This enables counsellors to have their own special attention and is of immense value in their formation. They have time to air their feelings and discuss their clients in private, away from any distractions arising from the network of relationships in the agency. Where such individual attention cannot be made available, a third option is shared supervision, for which two or three counsellors meet with the supervisor. Though not so intimate, this can prove an economical use of supervisor time, and enable peer support for the counsellors.

The supervisor–counsellor relationship has several features. For Foskett and Lyall (1988: 6) it is a partnership through which 'knowledge is imparted, experience compared, skills perfected, practice assessed and insight nurtured ... [it] contains the process of change, growth and development, together with all the attendant pressures and anxieties'. For Mearns (1991: 117–18) supervision has four basic conditions: commitment to a fully involved relationship; congruence through which the perceptions and insights of the supervisor can be used; valuing of the person being supervised; and empathy.

These are high requirements. It is easier in the voluntary sector to talk in ideal terms than to provide good enough supervision. Good supervisors are generally people with a great deal of experience and are hard to find. Many organizations do not have a tradition of paying supervisors and therefore rely on their voluntary commitment. Some are fortunate to be able to attract retired social workers whose experience is invaluable in supporting and guiding voluntary counsellors.

The more professionally minded organizations, like Relate and those associated with the Westminster Pastoral Foundation, have well-established supervision systems, often consisting of experienced counsellors from within their own ranks who have been given in-house training as supervisors. The supervisors themselves are provided with opportunities for regular group meetings with their colleagues, and for their own individual consultation sessions. These systems provide good support for the counsellors and the best means of developing their potential.

There is a danger that a supervisory system developed within an agency may foster a too uniform approach in counsellors. It is noteworthy that when the reasons for premature resignation of marriage counsellors was researched, one of the highest categories cited was conflict with supervisors (Heisler 1974). The implication was that supervisors as a group had too fixed a view of what was acceptable and were not making allowances for individual differences. Good supervision which nurtures the individual growth of counsellors is the most important factor in retaining volunteers for a long time.

At the other end of the scale in the voluntary sector, supervision can be haphazard. Supervisors may be drawn from a variety of disciplines, and thus bring in traditions from medical or pastoral care or even commercial management settings, in which practices of supervision may carry quite different connotations. At its best this can produce a dynamic and flexible atmosphere. More likely it means considerable unevenness, resulting in pot luck for the new counsellor.

At the very least it is important that every counsellor has a supervisor, and that counsellor and supervisor have made time to get to know each other and agree what to expect from their relationship. This means establishing a 'supervisory alliance' satisfactory to both parties (Hunt 1986). Supervisors should make clear their availability, especially if the time they can offer is limited, and they should not underestimate the anxiety that new counsellors may feel about approaching them. One young counsellor had been assigned a hospital doctor as a supervisor. He told her that she could ring him at any time at the hospital. The counsellor said:

> I made several attempts, but I always got his secretary, or an offer to bleep him, or I left messages which didn't get through. I gave up trying to contact him. Eventually we met and agreed to have a set time to ring. Now I ring him at home on Monday evenings and that works much better. I find that anything urgent can wait till then.

The guiding principle of supervision is that supervisors aim to strengthen counsellors in their work with their clients by nurturing their individual talents and personalities. They must not fall into the trap of directing them to work in the supervisor's way. They need to understand the constraints under which counsellors work, and the opportunities and drawbacks of being a voluntary counsellor. It is all too easy for competent practitioners working as supervisors, in effect, to take cases over themselves. Consciously, this is done by asking for the client to be referred to them. Unconsciously, it can be done at second hand by guiding the counsellor to work in the style of the supervisor, like a puppet on a string.

There are three basic elements in supervision. Proctor has described these as restorative, formative and normative (Hawkins and Shohet 1990: 42). The *restorative* or supportive function is of prime importance in the voluntary sector, where counsellors of goodwill but scant preparation find themselves heavily loaded with the unhappiness of their clients. 'I knew it was not going to be easy,' said a young nurse, newly trained as a bereavement counsellor, 'but I hadn't expected to feel so helpless. And I feel so alone without the support of the team I have in the hospital.' Her first client was older than she, but of an age and circumstances potentially to be a close friend.

> She was grieving the death of her twin sister. She had never come to terms with her sister marrying some years before, yet had always felt closer to her sister than her parents. I found myself deep in discussion about her relationship with her father, which really threw me as I realized I'd never thought about my father but had taken him for granted. This scared me. I felt out of my depth and I thought an older counsellor would be more help to her.

Her supervisor spent time talking through each encounter with her, giving her a hand to hold when feeling overwhelmed, and renewing her confidence to continue. The supervisor later commented: 'As with many of my new counsellors, she was doing a fine job and all I really needed to do was to hold her when her courage wavered and reassure her that she was doing well.'

Good supervision also entails a *formative* or educative element. The supervisor as teacher helps the counsellor to develop understanding and skill through intuitive questioning and prompting, by guided reading and experimentation. This implies a substantial commitment by supervisor and counsellor which is not always available in voluntary agencies. Where this standard of supervision is not provided, counsellors may, with justification, put pressure on their organizations. Some counsellors who are keen to improve their standard of practice pay for their own additional supervision elsewhere. Though the need may be greatest for supportive supervision in the early stages, the formative element is necessary to prevent counsellors becoming stale or stuck once they are established.

The third element is the *normative* or managerial one. As stated earlier, clients come first to an agency and only then to an individual counsellor, and the agency needs to check that the work done in its name is up to standard. The contract between agency and supervisor should make clear the supervisor's responsibility for ensuring that clients are getting 'good enough' service, that counsellors are not straying beyond the proper limits of agency practice and that the agency is not misusing its counsellors.

Agencies need to be clear about the roles and delegated responsibilities of supervisors. In voluntary organizations this is not easy, as many management committees have limited understanding of the nature of supervision. Some organizations have a formal channel of reporting back by supervisors to the management committee. This must take into account that, while supervisors have to ensure that standards of counselling are maintained, there is an element of confidentiality in the supervisor–counsellor relationship.

This is a sensitive area, and all too often channels of communication break down. Some committees are all too happy to pass the whole responsibility over to the supervisors. This is unsatisfactory because it means there is no procedure for dealing with crises when they occur, such as doubts about a counsellor's competence or complaints from clients. Some create sub-committees with responsibility for meeting as appropriate with the supervisors. That can ensure normal open two-way communication, and be the forum for tackling counselling or training problems in the organization before or after the event. If no such structure exists, it falls to the supervisors to ask for some procedure by which they can properly exercise their accountability to the management.

PAYMENT BY CLIENTS

'I was not worth paying for', laments one of the clients in the Isis centre (Oldfield 1983: 85). The centre is in the National Health Service, so clients are not charged. Yet, for that client, this did not prevent the issue of worth and payment arising.

'What's a few pounds to save a marriage?', asked one of Hunt's (1985) research sample. Another stated the dilemma he felt about having no fixed payment system:

I asked 'how much do people give?' and she said 'whatever you feel' which is awkward because you don't want to look

as if you are being mean when someone has given an hour
of their time, but then if you can't afford much . . .
                                        (Hunt 1985: 40)

Whether to have a fee or financial contribution, what sum to
suggest and how to collect it, are problematic issues. Many voluntary organizations find it difficult to institute a satisfactory system
of payments. Many counsellors and clients find it an embarrassing
subject.

The early counselling services acted on the assumption that counselling was free. Today only those who receive generous public
funding can still work on this premiss. Counselling was first seen as
part of the welfare state, available to all regardless of means. Counsellors gave their time without any thought of payment. Furthermore, counselling was not really understood by the public at large.
Writing in the late 1960s, Wallis (1968: 171) commented, 'even
to-day it is extremely difficult to convince people that such work is
worth paying for'.

In fact the first doubts that the service should be provided without charge were raised by psychiatrists who made a major input in
the training of counsellors. They observed that counsellors sometimes
had difficulties because their clients were uncommitted. They suggested that clients might value counselling more if they paid for it.
Instinctively, counsellors found it hard to respond positively to this
notion. Payment by clients seemed to undermine their need to give
service, and challenged them to assess what their counselling was
worth. The subject of payment rouses strong emotions, touching as
it does feelings about counsellors' self-worth. For a whole decade
marriage counsellors debated these issues and their effect upon the
therapeutic relationship.

Once payment for counselling became acceptable on therapeutic
grounds, financial considerations rapidly surfaced. With the cutting
back on public funds and grants to voluntary bodies, client contributions proved an effective way of bridging the shortfall. Gradually
the debate changed from whether clients should pay, to how to
produce a fee or donation system that was acceptable to counsellors
and clients and which did not discriminate against those who genuinely could not afford to make a contribution. In Australia the latter
problem has been solved by vouchers for counselling being issued
on request as part of the system of social security benefits. But in
the United Kingdom uncertainty and embarrassment on both sides
still arise with clients with inadequate means.

There are three possible ways of handling payments. Agencies which do not depend on fees may adopt a low-key approach, accepting donations offered or leaving a collecting box in a prominent place, but generally not pressing clients. A similar practice is followed by those agencies which do most of their counselling through home visits or by phone. Counsellors may then suggest at the termination of counselling that clients send a donation to their office.

The second approach is to ask counsellors to handle the question of payment with each client individually. This may be for practical reasons such as when counselling takes place away from an office, or when no administrative personnel are available. It may be because payment and the value put on the counselling are seen as important parts of the 'therapeutic alliance' which counsellors form with their clients. Many counsellors prefer to have the freedom to negotiate fees themselves. Where this practice is followed, clients need to be warned in advance that the rate of payment will be discussed and agreed during the course of counselling.

The third way is to treat the matter as a purely financial one and use office staff to collect fees before or after sessions, as happens in private medical or dental practices. Sometimes there is a set fee. More likely will be a sliding scale, with the cost of a session based on the client's income. For instance, the practice in the Swindon Counselling Service is to charge a set fee for the initial assessment interview which all referrals receive. In 1992 this was £15. At that interview one of the matters raised is the client's financial situation, and a contribution is then settled for each counselling session, between £1 and the amount charged for the initial interview. The intake worker aims for a fair price which neither undervalues the service nor commits clients to a cost which later turns out to be unrealistically high for them. A different system puts responsibility on clients at the outset by giving them a grid showing income brackets and suggested fee, and asking them to locate their financial position on it and determine their own level of contribution.

Counselling touches closely on feelings of self-worth, on both sides of the counselling relationship. Counsellors often feel undervalued by their organizations. Agencies can feel unsupported by their communities. Clients come with feelings of worthlessness. Many counsellors and befrienders underestimate their importance to their clients. Those who are confident in their counselling succeed in handling these financial questions without embarrassment.

It is small wonder, though, that questions of value and worth are close to the surface in voluntary organizations. Many have a continual struggle to survive, and succeed in working wonders on low budgets. All are heavily dependent on voluntary endeavour. Volunteers are the main resource of most agencies. The next chapter will consider how these resources are managed, and in particular how the voluntary sector goes about the task of organizing the recruitment, training and deployment of its volunteers.

· FOUR ·

Specific issues in counselling in the voluntary sector

TYPE AND SIZE OF AGENCY

'The best is the enemy of the good' is an apposite aphorism for voluntary counselling agencies to remember. Most of them know only too well that they have limitations. Rarely can you talk with members of a counselling service without their mentioning their aspirations – the hope to open for longer hours, to put their part-time administrator on a salary scale, to recruit more counsellors, to start group work with clients, to acquire new chairs, to set up outposts in isolated housing estates, to get a local authority grant, to establish a central office, to cut down the waiting list, to have better contacts with local doctors, to become computerized, to strengthen the management committee, to attract the young or the black or the disabled or the men or the single mothers, and so on.

Feelings of inadequacy are more common than a sense of complacency. There is a widespread awareness of the need to provide a service which, in Winnicott's (1965) much-used phrase in relation to mothering, is 'good enough'. These aspirations to improve are admirable. Without them agencies merely stagnate. But a balance always has to be struck between standards which are good enough, and those which are so demanding of people and resources that they become counter-productive.

A significant factor determining the standard of service is the size of the agency. At one extreme are small autonomous local counselling agencies, likely to be dependent on one or more key figures, such as their organizers and/or chairpersons. They are often examples of 'small is beautiful'. Everyone knows everyone; a team spirit and trust are likely to develop; and, at its best, everything functions well. One such agency has eight counsellors and is funded by a local authority. The person who is the driving force behind it is organizer and trainer, supervisor and receptionist. In her own words, she disbanded the management committee as it was more of a liability than a help, and she relies for support on the responsible local government officer. The agency has a very good reputation, but clearly there is a danger that too much is dependent on the health and continued commitment of the one individual.

Where agencies are bigger, or are members of a large network, there is greater need for the distribution of power and sharing of responsibility for monitoring performance. Many management committees find it useful to have a counselling sub-committee whose remit it is to develop and maintain standards of counselling, sometimes also with responsibility for selecting counsellors and allocating cases. Training can also be part of the remit of such a counselling committee or can be given over to a different working group. Where responsibility for the technical work is devolved in this way, it is important for it not to be cut off from the administration. Such a split is not uncommon and can bring in its wake lack of trust and bad feelings on both sides. A regular system of reporting back to the management committee must be instituted, as the final responsibility for the service rests with the management committee.

Where there is a national network the headquarters exercises a monitoring function. The Westminster Pastoral Foundation, for instance, has a two-tier system. Organizations first become affiliates of the Foundation, receiving advice and guidance from the parent body. When they consider they have achieved the requisite standard, they apply to become associate members. This involves an extensive inspection of all aspects of their service by an appropriate member of the Foundation. If associate membership is granted, further inspections are carried out on a regular basis.

The Samaritans also has a system for monitoring its network. It arranges for intensive branch reviews to be undertaken triennially by a team of volunteers from other branches, who are specially selected for the task. The National Association of Bereavement Services, which was founded in 1988 as an umbrella body for independent agencies, aims to introduce a similar system in its network. Agencies which have no parent body can usefully arrange their own reviews on similar lines by inviting occasional formal scrutiny from experienced members of other counselling bodies. It might well be advantageous for them to collaborate in establishing their own formal system for mutual monitoring.

Some national organizations have a network of paid staff

throughout Britain, with titles such as 'development officer', 'area organizer' or 'regional manager'. They have responsibility for ensuring that the local groups continue to provide a good enough service. Most of these staff members are in frequent touch with all their local groups and visit them at least once a year. They use a mixture of stick and carrot techniques. Their visits may be welcomed or feared. Their ultimate aim is to assist the local group in assessing its own performance and setting realistic objectives for the year ahead.

This exercise of control by a central body is not without its tensions. The strength of the system lies in the support, stimulus and challenge it gives to local groups. Problems arise where local groups feel too much is demanded of them – frequently expressed in such words as 'It's all very well for those paid staff down in London, but they've got no idea what its like for us here in this town'. There are often conflicts when the central staff member feels that a group has the wrong sort of people managing it and that change needs to be brought about. Such conflict arises particularly in organizations like Relate, where a strong central control is kept over the technical side of the work through a nationally organized selection, training and supervision system; yet the local group has responsibility for administration and finance. The local management can claim, with some justification, that it is required to resource its counsellors yet has no control over the way they work.

In reality, standards vary in different parts of Britain. For instance, there is a North–South divide in counselling as in many other aspects of life. The average agency in the South is wealthier than its counterpart in the North, not only in terms of finance but also in personnel and resources of all sorts. Then there are differences between urban and rural areas. It is possible to recruit volunteers in rural areas, but it is more difficult than in denser urban areas to deploy them efficiently and give them extensive experience. Counsellor availability varies greatly. Volunteers with counselling potential are easier to recruit in places with substantial middle-class populations, supported by lively tertiary educational establishments. The resources to fund offices and equipment are hard to come by in depressed parts of Britain.

Agencies also acquire their own local characteristics. These may be historical, stemming from the group of individuals who were the founder members. Others come in time to be dominated by one section of the community, and acquire the particular flavour and interests of that group. One service may be thought to be the preserve of a university counselling course, another of feminists or of a particular local church. These local feelings of uniqueness are often strong. They may provide the dynamic for an agency, but such parochialism limits the appeal of the service to the general public.

Looking at the United Kingdom as a whole, national feelings also have to be taken into account. Some larger bodies have their own separate structures for England, Scotland, Wales and Northern Ireland. Others struggle to devolve powers to the separate nations while still keeping central control. Such a mix is not easy. Time and massive travelling expenses can torpedo attempts at regular close working relationships. The Scottish Association of Counselling, for example, has a precarious history of trying to maintain a separate existence from BAC. Northern Ireland has its own association. So far one is not yet envisaged in Wales.

The size of population and geographical spread in both Wales and Northern Ireland make it difficult for the large counselling organizations to establish separate autonomous bodies there. As there is only the potential for a small number of branches in either country, it is difficult, though not impossible, for them to establish their own independent national bodies. Some organizations, such as the Irish Catholic Marriage Advisory Council, cover the whole of Ireland.

These national variations pose real structural headaches. At their core, however, is the need to give full recognition to the unique identities and characteristics of the nations within the British Isles. In Wales this includes the importance of recruiting bilingual staff and counsellors. The large nation-wide bodies have the challenge of fostering these national variations, while at the same time capitalizing on the benefits which flow from preserving the solidarity of a common presence across the whole of the United Kingdom.

MANAGING AGENCIES

The responsibility for running voluntary organizations is normally vested in a management committee or a group of trustees. Many take this responsibility extremely seriously and keep a close watch over all activities. Some meet infrequently and leave the running of business to paid staff. In rare instances, a management committee of voluntary members may have ceased to function adequately and its powers may be exercised by a responsible officer.

In counselling organizations management is often an unpopular task. Many groups now report more difficulty in recruiting committee members than counsellors. People attracted to the counselling sphere feel, not surprisingly, that the essential nature of the work lies in face-to-face contact. Satisfaction comes from the feeling of giving

direct personal help to someone. The satisfactions of being part of
the management are less easy to appreciate. Managers who are
attuned to commercial business practices can find it frustrating to
work in the apparently non-directive world of the counsellor, who
tends to take things at the client's pace.

A management committee carries out what A.K. Rice calls the
'boundary' function. It has the internal task of enabling the service
to run efficiently. This may include mediating between conflicting
interests within the agency, or at least, in Rice's words, ensuring
that the right people are fighting each other about the right things
(Miller and Rice 1967). It also has the function of answering to its
external supporters, funding bodies, the local community, and so
on.

The committee should be constituted so that it can carry out
these diverse tasks. It should have on it a representative from local
government or the health authority, and perhaps members from
colleague organizations such as CABx, volunteer bureaux or the
Samaritans. Valauble contributions can also be made by people from
caring professions, the churches, Rotary or Round Table, local media
or sympathetic individuals of some standing in the community.

These external representatives bring goodwill and commitment,
but in practice they often find it difficult to know how to contribute
to day-to-day business. Care needs to be taken to induct new members. All too often it is assumed they know far more about what the
organization actually does than is the case. They may find themselves involved in decisions about matters they do not understand,
or feel frustrated that their talents are underused. It requires sensitive chairing to nurture their commitment and make best use of
their potentially valuable contribution on the committee.

Internal members on the committee come from the agency's own
administrative personnel, the counsellors and any other voluntary
helpers. A frequent practice is for the counsellors to elect one or
two of their number to represent them on the committee. These
internal members know what the agency is all about and, unless
they make a conscious effort to inform the external members, they
can dominate the business proceedings. Some local organizations
reach the point where their committees are comprised only of internal members. Though this may well serve to expedite business,
it often results in the maintenance of the status quo, and, more
dangerously, in becoming cut off from the outside community. This
can be particularly unfortunate when hard times strike, as the local
community may then be ill informed about the agency and less
inclined to give sympathetic support. Time-consuming and trying

though it is, the effort is important to maintain a well-balanced committee which can exploit this boundary more fully.

The same considerations apply on a national scale with the large network counselling organizations. They have a formal democratic electoral system which attempts to ensure that regions and different internal interests are adequately represented. Here the central management committee not only carries out the boundary function between the external environment and the inner world of the agency, but also mediates the boundary between the central headquarters and the local constituent groups. External members may be co-opted on to the committee, and relevant national government departments may send representatives who attend under the somewhat threatening label of 'observers'. Again, this external presence needs to be nurtured, as at local level, lest the internal politics tends to dominate proceedings.

As these nation-wide counselling organizations have grown, their management committees have undergone various constitutional changes. The founder members, most of them prestigious people who retain influential roles for many years, have been superseded by people elected from local branches. In both NMGC and Cruse it took thirty years for the chair of the management committee to pass from a national figure to someone elected from the shop floor, so to speak, of a local branch.

These changes have made the organizations more truly democratic. There is now less feeling that everything is dominated by a central group based in London and out of touch with the rest of Britain. However, national committees composed of local representatives have their own drawbacks. Many of those who play a full part in a local branch are bewildered by the scale of business at national level, and find themselves trying to grapple inadequately with issues they cannot understand from their experience of branches in their own locality. The business of a national committee may seem light years away from grassroots counselling.

Even in small counselling organizations or local branches there are conflicting interests which give rise to what Rice calls 'fights' (Miller and Rice 1967). Counsellors have a particular loyalty to their clients. Those who work in the office, whether salaried or not, are most aware of the clients who cannot be offered help and of the length of the waiting list. Trainers may value quality rather than quantity; they tend to look with disfavour on counsellors who get through clients too quickly, even though such throughput may delight the appointments secretary! The treasurer and publicity officer are more conscious of the agency's external image and the need to meet the expectations of funding bodies. And on top of all that, national headquarters may be making additional demands which threaten to overstretch local resources!

In his thorough study of the management of voluntary organizations, Charles Handy (1988) adapts Belbin's (1981) categorization of eight roles necessary to a committee. He allows that any two, rarely more, can be carried by one individual. He calls these roles the chairperson, who is essentially the co-ordinator of the committee; the shaper, who possesses the drive to be a task leader; the plant, who is the person with ideas; the monitor/evaluator, who asks critical questions; the resource investigator, who brings new contacts; the company worker, who turns ideas into plans; the team worker, who builds bridges between groups; and the finisher, who worries about deadlines and completion (Handy 1988: 56).

The management committees of all counselling agencies need to fulfil these roles. In practice, committees are composed of people who come together from a mixture of local historical development, personal contacts and expediency, and there may be serious gaps. A strong committee has an awareness of different people performing each role. In many groups, however, too much falls on one or two willing horses. Handy commends the voluntary sector for its preference for participative and democratic ways of working. But he sounds a warning which should not be ignored by committees of management: that achieving these several tasks requires conscious attention and should not be left to chance (Handy 1988: 64).

RECRUITING COUNSELLORS

Just as football team managers emphasize the importance of the team but pay out most for the strikers who have to score the goals, so counselling agencies value all members of their team but place most emphasis on getting the right counsellors. In Cruse, for instance, the appointment of telephone contacts, social group organizers, committee members, organizing secretaries and treasurers is all left to local initiative. Only for the selection of counsellors are clear guidelines of policy and practice laid down for all branches to follow.

Cruse is not alone in differentiating counsellors in such fashion. It is clear historically why this has come about. Without counsellors a service cannot be set up, and so counsellors become the biggest asset. The unfortunate by-product is that counsellors thus acquire a status which can excite envy and which undervalues the other members of the team.

Agencies have various ways of recruiting their counsellors. Some, for example Feltham Open Door, anticipate vacancies which are to occur in their counselling force and advertise throughout the locality, finally selecting on a competitive basis from a short list of applicants. Some, for example Wantage Counselling Service, have enough unsolicited applicants to take rather more than they need on their three-year training course. At the end of the first year a selection process is held and trainees who opt to continue and are assessed to be suitable complete the next two years of the course. Relate branches are always on the look-out for suitable counsellors and at any time can send forward candidates with potential to the national selection scheme. Cruse policy is to run an open course in all branches annually, as an introduction to bereavement; and then to invite applications from people who complete the course satisfactorily. A formal selection process then takes place both before and after completion of a further course on counselling skills. Victim Support branches run an introductory course when they have enough volunteers interested in becoming visitors.

Whatever the system in each agency, selection ought to be seen not as a one-off event, but as one significant stage of a continuous assessment process. Furthermore, it is a two-way process in which candidates are making their assessment of their own ability and of the agency. They are learning more about counselling and what will be expected of them. At any stage they may decide that counselling is not for them, or that they would not fit into the agency, and pull out. At one time there was a 10% drop-out rate of marriage counsellor candidates between being selected for training and actually embarking on it. That seemed a healthy phenomenon, as there can be a big gap between the expectations of candidates and the reality they encounter in training and at work, and it is better that they realize this earlier rather than later.

Some agencies expect their new recruits or students to complete basic training before beginning counselling. It is more common for trainees to begin counselling under close supervision at some stage during training, so that the formation of the counsellor is through a mixture of theory and practice. Relate counsellors begin work after the second of their six residential training sessions. In one local service counsellors begin at the end of their first year. In less developed agencies, especially where there is pressure to attend to clients, counsellors may begin working after a fairly rudimentary basic training, in the belief that, being the right sort of people, they will learn on the job.

There are great differences in how agencies approach the

appointment of counsellors. These variations reflect how the agencies view the counselling task. Some of them rely on the good-will and sense of their recruits and do not spell out what is required of them. Mostly this works well enough, but at times it leads to misunderstandings and disappointment for the agency or counsellor when there is a mismatch in the expectations each has of the other. Those agencies which emphasize the need for formal contracts between clients and counsellors are also likely to have formal terms of service for potential counsellors. The Brook Advisory Centres, for instance, produce a set contract for their counsellors. This includes what is expected from them in terms of hours worked and their relationship with the management.

It is good practice to draw up such a contract. It is also important to monitor that the terms are being fulfilled. Such monitoring is more easy to carry out in agencies which have a competent administrative back-up. Nevertheless, even the smallest agency will find it worthwhile to draw up a simple specification for its counsellors.

The duties and obligations of the counsellor and the agency can be written down and signed by both parties. The counsellor under-takes to:

(i)   do so many sessions of counselling;
(ii) attend in-service training;
(iii) attend individual or group supervision (some agencies specify at least two-thirds attendance is required);
(iv) comply with agency practice in relation to note-taking and confidentiality;
(v)   observe any other local requirements.

The agency may undertake to:

(i)   provide a set amount of training and supervision sessions;
(ii) allocate clients within local limits;
(iii) arrange insurance cover for the counsellor;
(iv) reimburse expenses and, if relevant, make agreed payments.

The objections to introducing such contracts centre on the fear that an agency may not be able to fulfil its part of the bargain. Some agency statements about the supervision they will provide are hon-oured more in the breach than the observance! Many organizations are tentative about their volunteers. 'They are only volunteers and you can not push them too far' is a frequent belief. This is, I suggest, a mistaken attitude. Volunteers wish to be taken seriously and to be valued. Nothing is more frustrating than volunteering for a job and being underused. Personal satisfaction lies in being treated as someone with a potential that needs to be developed and used to the good of the community. Experience bears out that the more that is demanded of volunteers by way of a professional attitude, the more they rise to the occasion.

In this also lies the clue to recruiting volunteers. The days are now past when advertising for volunteers sounded apologetic: 'Can you spare a little time? Please help a good cause.' Today it is recognized that, in addition to wanting to give service to the community, volunteers are seeking to gain something for themselves. Recruitment policy can address those needs openly: 'Join our team. Learn a new skill. We offer you training and support as a counsellor. A unique opportunity to improve yourself as well as give service to the community.'

This acknowledges that the recruit is offered recompense, not financial, but through a sense of belonging to a significant group and through the opportunity for personal development which may lead to new career potential. Such advertising reflects the determination of the agency to treat its volunteers seriously, as if they were paid employees, and sets the tone for their training and deployment in the organization.

SELECTING COUNSELLORS

'Samaritans are born not made', begins the Samaritans' training manual (Vining 1981: 1). It goes on to say that there are varied views within the organization as to the quantity and quality of training that such 'naturals' require; but there is agreement that training can only develop potential. It cannot create it. The potential for Samaritans is identified as resting in four qualities:

(i)   caring;
(ii) willingness to share a caller's suffering;
(iii) the emotional strength to bear that suffering;
(iv) the ability to respond with sensitivity and acceptance.

These qualities hold true throughout the voluntary counselling sector. Those responsible for selection emphasize that it is first and foremost personal qualities that they are looking for, not academic qualifications or specialist experience. The hairdresser who hears many confidences and the young mother who finds people at the school gates want to talk about their troubles, stand more chance of passing the selection process than the lecturer in sociology or the store manager. Sometimes the very individuals who might be thought to make natural counsellors, because they are already dealing with people in difficulties, find it most difficult to adapt. Home carers, doctors, nurses and others whose work frequently requires active help and problem-solving may well have ingrained patterns of caring and feel uncomfortable with the more passive stance involved in counselling.

Because selection consists of assessing personal characteristics it is fraught with difficulty. Selectors can easily fall prey to their own blindspots or prejudices. The first essential is to have a process in which assessment is carried out by a team, so that responsibility is shared. Selectors are likely to be agreed about the candidates who are naturals, and those who are clearly unsuitable. However, there are bound to be borderline candidates who are difficult to assess. They often evoke different reactions in the selectors. It is essential to have time to discuss the strengths and weaknesses of such candidates freely in order to share these difficult decisions and reach a common view.

In most voluntary counselling agencies selection entails interviews with individual selectors, and probably a session with a panel. Ideally the selectors are a mixture of people chosen from inside the agency, with one or two external selectors to provide a detached viewpoint. The latter may have a role in challenging assumptions about the range of candidates who are acceptable.

It is important that references are taken up. It may be stipulated that at least one of the referees should know the candidate well – a long-standing next-door neighbour's comments can be more helpful than those of a distant boss or local vicar. Some agencies send a detailed form with open-ended questions to each referee asking, among other questions, what qualities the applicant would bring to counselling and what snags might arise for them as counsellors. Though such forms sometimes elicit superficial glowing tributes, they are mainly taken very conscientiously. It is not uncommon for referees to express reservations about the candidate. Research into selection outcomes and the subsequent performance of successful candidates has shown that doubts expressed by referees were to a large extent well founded and should have been heeded (Heisler 1977).

Relate has a long-established selection system organized on a national basis with meticulous care. At one time selection lasted two days, either on a residential basis or as two separate one-day events. Now a full day is given over to a selection conference. At each event there are eight candidates and three selectors. These candidates have already had a preliminary vetting locally, after which the local branch only sponsors for national selection those candidates whom they judge to have good potential.

The intensive selection day comprises group discussion, observed by the selectors; two individual interviews; and some written work, including a self-description which is invariably revealing. Objective intelligence tests have been used, but, because of time constraints, they have not been found to provide sufficient relevant information about the candidates.

Such a comprehensive process of selection in groups is beyond the resources of most voluntary agencies. The norm elsewhere is individual interviews with applicants. But whatever the procedure, selectors are seeking for the same qualities in their recruits and need to bring to the task the same thoroughness and objectivity. The principal qualities were spelt out in a reseach study in 1967 in the United States and were mentioned in Chapter 1: genuineness, non-possessive warmth and accurate empathy (Truax and Carkhuff 1967). A quarter-century later, these are still the qualities sought by selectors.

It is also of fundamental importance for selectors to ascertain that candidates are relatively at ease with themselves and comfortable enough with their lifestyle. For instance, those offering themselves for work in organizations dealing with sexual issues need to be confident about their own sexual orientation, whether that is homosexual, heterosexual or bisexual. In couple counselling, candidates need to be at ease with their singleness, divorced state, marriage or other partnership, because they will find that working with clients may cause them to see their own relationships in a new light. A single person who yearns for marriage and children, or a married person feeling trapped in a loveless marriage, or a divorcee still resentful about separation, will find it hard to be open to the pain of others. The person who has not come to terms with her own loss is unlikely to be able to cope well with other people's bereavement. As Raphael (1984: 401) observes:

> empathy with the bereaved in their encounters with loss and death touches off in each one of us the most personal of terrors. We all have to learn to live with loss, but the person who works in this sphere must confront it every day.

Selectors might wish they had the wisdom of Solomon. In practice, whatever the system, the difficulties remain much as they were years ago when Paul Halmos (1965: 163) wrote:

The paradox in selection is well known. We want sane counsellors, but we want them also a little neurotic; we want them
to be sensitive yet impervious to the emotional provocations
of the job; we want them to be intelligent but we don't want
them to be intellectuals who tend to be, and can be, artisti-
cally or scientifically rebellious, or just seemingly critical.

For him a requisite of what he called 'the faith of the counsellors'
was 'the even-tempered acceptance of contradictions, the calm tol-
erance of uncertainty and dissention' (Halmos 1965: 173). He might
have added that the same faith is a requirement in selectors.

Agencies are seeking accurately to assess candidates' present
capacity, and their potential for continuing growth through training. They also have to reject those who are not suitable. This often
causes anxiety for the agency and pain for the candidate. The selection process may help to clarify for applicants that counselling is
not the right sort of work for them. Some selectors hint at this
during their individual interviews. But it is common for candidates
to feel rejected when they learn that their hopes of becoming a
counsellor are not realized.

It is possible to try to soften the blow by suggesting that the
applicant takes on a different role in the organization. However,
this can be unwise. It is better for unaccepted candidates to move
away for a time to come to terms with their disappointment. They
might be be told what other opportunities are available if they ask,
and advised to return in a few months. Failed counsellors who have
not accepted the verdict but who then stay on in some other role
may feel unfulfilled in themselves and can be awkward colleagues
for all concerned.

How much should candidates be told the reasons why they were
not accepted? The ideal is, of course, to be open; indeed, some
agencies offer personal interviews to those who are not accepted to
discuss the reasons. In practice, though, this is extremely time-
consuming and may lead to lengthy interchanges which can become
acrimonious. Agencies must also respect the confidentiality of the
referees, whose opinions must not be divulged. An agency's actual
responsibility is limited to deciding whether or not to take an applicant, in the same way as any other employer.

Given the time constraints, a straight letter which thanks the
applicant for coming but states that they have not been accepted
may be all that the agency is able to say. This is not in the best
style of counselling, and some applicants will be left bruised by too
businesslike a letter. It is difficult to get the balance right, especially

when informing someone who has already been assessed as lacking insight and self-awareness. There is no easy system. However it is dressed up, rejecting a volunteer is an unpleasant task. What must be borne in mind is that the first responsibility of the recruiting body is to its clients, so selectors must ensure as far as they can that future clients are not exposed to people who have been wrongly selected as counsellors.

TRAINING COUNSELLORS

Whatever its length and intensity, there are three distinct parts to the training of counsellors: knowledge and information have to be acquired; personal understanding and sensitivity need to be developed; and counselling skills must be learned and practised.

Agencies vary greatly in the weight that they give to these three parts. Some concentrate at first on experiential training to increase trainees' sensitivity. Some launch straight into counselling, and believe that relevant information and sensitivity can be acquired by practice. Some lay store on a grounding in theory. There are variations also in what is considered appropriate to cover in basic training and what is best left for in-service training once trainees have begun to gain counselling experience.

The knowledge needed includes information about the organization itself, its purpose, history perhaps, and present structure, personnel and clients, the availability of referral agencies, and so on. A basic understanding of the phenomenon of the particular client group with which the agency deals is necessary, be it substance abuse, bereavement, relationships, sexual functioning or other specialities. Human growth and development may feature in the programme. The temptation of in-house courses is to include too much academic study, and to keep adding to it as new issues emerge.

Second, there is the need for experiential training, which is important to enable counsellors to develop insight and personal understanding on which their empathy in the counselling room is based. They need to learn about what Jacobs (1985) calls their own 'presenting past'. Training must present them with opportunities to learn more about themselves, their formative influences, their beliefs and prejudices, their ability to cope with pain, anger and silence, and how their colleagues see them. Group work generally features largely in this sort of training. It includes discussion, role-play and simulated counselling. In this way, for instance, counsellors preparing to work with disabled clients test out their own attitudes to disabled people, explore their assumptions, act out situations in which they sense what it is like to be limbless or, in Segal's (1991: 335) words, feeling 'bad' and 'avoided like the plague'.

Third, counsellors are taught what are known as *counselling skills*. These are their professional box of tools. It is commonplace now to start by introducing counsellors to a conceptual framework of counselling such as devised by Egan (1986). This describes three stages in counselling: exploration of the problem; understanding; action. The skills appropriate for the first stage will be concerned with how to listen, how to probe, how to paraphrase, and how to empathize. The second-stage skills may concern how to reflect feelings and make connections, how to challenge and how to summarize. And the skills for the third stage will relate to how to make assessments and evaluations, how to make plans and how to finish the counselling relationship. These skills can be taught in the classroom. They are useful for the beginner, if not used too self-consciously. Like any other skill, however, they work best when they are used spontaneously because they have been thoroughly integrated into the natural response of the practitioner.

Many voluntary organizations, which have only a limited number of days or weeks rather than years to prepare their counsellors, find it most effective to train them in small groups, ideally comprising eight to twelve trainees and either one or two trainers. Such groups become safe places for sharing experience and insights, for openness in reacting to each other, and learning from trainers, group members and specialist tutors. It is important to remember that nobody is an absolute beginner. Everyone has relevant experience to bring to the group, perhaps of being a helper or of having been a client; perhaps memories, sad or happy, as a child, parent, lover, manager, subordinate or victim; perhaps of having been on the receiving end of immigration procedures, imprisonment or hospitalization; perhaps of feeling suicidal. A skilful trainer draws on the wealth of emotional experiences in the group and channels them into the formation of each trainee.

Trainers may be home-grown or imported, and probably paid, to undertake specific parts of the training. Increasingly organizations are encouraging their counsellors to take additional external training, perhaps with the Open University or at a local tertiary education college. Such courses can give counsellors a broader vision beyond their own specialist clientele. They enable counsellors to learn from people working in other settings, and test themselves against them. This is particularly valuable once counsellors have acquired confidence in their own agency.

Trainers working in an experiential mode continually draw parallels between the trainer–trainee relationship and the counsellor–client one. Both are relationships which explore together in a trusting atmosphere for intuition and enlightenment. Sensitive trainers are seen as something of a model by the new counsellor. It is highly desirable that the trainers have a deep understanding of counselling in the agency, preferably based in continuing practice. If, perforce, the main trainer is from outside and not steeped in the culture of the agency, a joint training role with someone less skilled as a trainer but with the insider's touch can prove advantageous.

It must be clear to the agency and the students whether, or to what extent, an initial training course is used as an instrument for selection. There is a dilemma here for voluntary organizations with few resources. If the organization feels that its selection process is not very thorough, it is fair to stipulate that further selection will take place after training and that the trainers will be asked for their assessments of the trainees. But this must be stated openly. It is not satisfactory that trainees who think they have been accepted participate in training groups where they respond without inhibition to the group leader's encouragement to express emotions, take risks and reveal their innermost thoughts, only to find that, unbeknown to them, the trainers report back as a form of secondary selection to selectors.

One great strength of the voluntary sector is that it is possible to control the speed at which training and practice are integrated. Counselling is *par excellence* a craft which is learnt by doing. In my opinion, the sooner practical experience can be gained by the novice the better. Later aspects of basic training are then grounded in the experience that trainees bring back to the group. Clients are no longer an unknown but a reality, making it possible for the group members to focus on real live issues.

Such practice is not damaging to clients. Although it may appear to be using them as guinea-pigs, research findings do not confirm such doubts. Hunt (1985: 48) found that there was no correlation between whether clients felt helped or were satisfied or otherwise, and whether their counsellors were fully trained or in training. Often the same fully trained counsellor or counsellor in training could appear to have helped one client and not helped another client. It seems that what the one group of counsellors possesses in experience and know-how, the other beginning group makes up for in enthusiasm and undivided attention to the client.

However short or extended the basic training, voluntary organizations need to accept the principle of continuous in-service training. In some agencies this is more or less synonymous with regular supervision, especially in groups. The supervisor can decide with the group how to allocate sessions. Most are given over to discussion of current cases, but some sessions focus on a topic, perhaps with a visiting expert, or take the form of a book review.

An alternative is periodically to set aside time in an evening or at a weekend for all the counsellors to meet together to explore a theme, such as child sex abuse, racial harassment or HIV/AIDS. Such meetings fulfil other purposes. They can be used for business, such as designing an improved record sheet, for airing grievances or for discussing aspects of the organization's policy. A very important purpose is also for social gathering. Agencies need to remember, with the writer of Ecclesiastes, that there is 'a time to weep and a time to laugh; a time to mourn and a time to dance'. It does not have to be all work.

ACCREDITATION OF COUNSELLORS

The steady move towards the professionalization of counselling shows up nowhere more clearly than in the issue of accreditation. The organizations in membership of BAC have been grappling with these issues for two decades. They have argued the pros and cons of whether priority should be given to creating a scheme for granting recognition to individual counsellors, or to supervisors or to the courses offering training. The debate has been sharpened by EC requirements aiming at common standards throughout Europe. The standards currently being set nationally are beyond the reach of nearly all in the voluntary sector in Britain. So voluntary agencies are themselves left with the question of what sort of in-house accreditation system to introduce.

Many agencies are not concerned about formal recognition for counsellors. What is important for them is that their counsellors are competent. The fact that they are working acceptably within the organization is, for them, recognition enough. They consider that producing their own internal certificate would not mean anything outside the agency and, to be of any value internally, would need regular updating, which is a time-consuming and expensive process.

Counsellors themselves are increasingly seeing things rather differently. More and more voluntary counsellors set their sights on a professional career or quasi-professional role. For them a certificate contains a measure of assessment of competence and acknowledgement of their experience. They welcome any help with their aspirations. As for the agency itself, the award of a certificate of competence is at the very least an accolade to its counsellors and a significant gesture of thanks for their voluntary contribution.

More agencies are therefore finding ways of accrediting their counsellors. Sometimes it is by issuing a certificate at the end of basic training, stating that the course has been satisfactorily completed. More usually it is by providing a certificate at the end of a probationary period, acknowledging that competence as a counsellor depends on the exercise of the skills and insights acquired during training. Cruse, for example, issues a certificate to counsellors who have passed basic training; completed 60 hours of counselling; completed 20 hours of group and individual supervision; and satisfied their supervisors that they have acquired the necessary standard of skill and knowledge.

Other organizations require more extensive experience for a certificate of accreditation. Some are working to introduce a regular process of assessment every three years or so. Underlying these innovations is the concern of the organizations not only to raise standards but also to attempt to retain counsellors by providing internal incentives. Most voluntary agencies have no career ladder. A voluntary counsellor seldom moves beyond being a counsellor, so it is valuable for the organization to recognize a person's length of service. In more developed agencies experienced counsellors can apply to become supervisors or trainers, or move into paid administrative posts. The growing practice in Relate, for instance, is to pay counsellors a sessional fee for undertaking interviews over and above their voluntary commitment. However, in most agencies, those who want to remain counsellors and develop their range of work have to look outside to extend themselves.

It is not surprising that turnover rates among counsellors are high. Detailed statistics are not easy to obtain, but a voluntary agency is fortunate if it keeps its counsellors on average for three years. Some counsellors use the training in voluntary organizations quite consciously as a step towards a professional post. Others, particularly women whose children are growing up and are thinking of returning to paid work, find that the counselling they embarked on as a part-time activity holds for them the attraction of a second career in which they can capitalize on their experience of the dynamics of family relationships. As far back as 1958, John Wallis in Marriage Guidance was complaining that recruiting counsellors was like trying to fill a bucket with holes in it – and those were days when many middle-class women had no aspiration for paid employment! The bucket has become no easier to fill over the years. The main consolation for those of us involved in the recruitment of counsellors is that the loss to the voluntary agencies that provided the training has proved the gain of the community at large. Many of those who do resign earlier than their agencies would wish move into the caring professions, or into other fields where they make use of the counselling expertise they have acquired.

Of greater concern to the agencies than these 'upwardly mobile' losses are those counsellors who leave for other reasons, such as stress, feelings of inadequacy, or dissatisfaction. To avoid this wastage, as discussed in Chapter 3, agencies must provide a high standard of supervision. Many agencies fall short in this regard. They have a high turnover rate of counsellors and spend much time on recruiting and training new ones. Some would be well advised to reallocate the time and effort they presently spend on recruitment to strengthening their supervisory system. They would then increase the likelihood of holding on to their current counsellors.

CLIENT ASSESSMENT

There is no universal procedure in voluntary counselling organizations for responding to new clients. Some agencies spend time on the telephone trying to get an impression of the client's needs so that an appropriate counsellor can be allocated. Others, in particular the generic agencies, place great emphasis on assessment and invite clients for a first interview specifically for this purpose. In contrast, many of the specialist agencies have no specific assessment procedure. They are likely to allocate clients to a counselllor who has an immediate vacancy, rather than try for a careful match of client with counsellor.

A sophisticated intake procedure is not possible in situations where there is either no office or a rarely staffed one; or where there is severe shortage of counsellors; or, frankly, a lack of necessary skills for conducting proper diagnostic interviews. For all agencies there is a danger of duplication of effort. Clients can be faced with the irksome prospect of starting to tell their story all over a second time. Agencies can feel that this is not the best use of counsellor time.

Some counsellors are also against assessment interviews on principle. They consider that the initial contact between counsellor and client is a crucial bonding element in creating the therapeutic alliance between them, and that counselling starts the moment they first meet. They feel that any earlier intervention by a third party, however skilfully handled, has the effect of distorting that first meeting. Furthermore, the client might form an immediate rapport with the assessment interviewer and view allocation to another counsellor as a poor substitute.

A first assessment interview is held in many of the generic agencies. This can be conducted, as in Feltham Open Door, by a counselling co-ordinator who knows the abilities, skills and strengths of all members of the counselling team. There are several advantages to such a system. It generally means that enquirers can be seen initially within a few days for their first contact, even if there is subsequently a considerable time-lag before they can start their counselling.

More importantly, this first interview acts as a two-way process in assisting the client to decide whether the agency is the right place to come for help. Even where only 20 minutes are allowed for each assessment, sufficient information can be imparted for potential clients to learn about the agency, while the interviewer can assess whether the agency is best able to meet the client's needs. Assessors need to weigh up not only whether counselling is likely to be a suitable form of help, but also whether the waiting time for it can be tolerated and, in fee-paying services, whether the financial arrangements will be acceptable.

An assessment interview needs to discern clients' reasons for coming and an outline of their problems. Clients should be asked what previous sort of help they have received, who, if anyone, advised them to come and what their hopes and expectations are. On the basis of such information the interviewer decides whether to offer ongoing counselling and may already have in mind which counsellor would be most appropriate.

Intake interviews of this sort are quite different from counselling sessions. Assessors have clear short-term goals. They are likely to be warm and empathetic, but need to discourage too dependent a relationship being formed. New clients often have a strong urge to unburden pent-up feelings. The skill of intake interviewing is helping clients to contain their feelings sufficiently while stating enough of their problem for a diagnostic assessment to be made. This goes so much against the grain of client-centred counselling that counsellors trained in that mode find it hard to achieve. The temptation to start counselling has to be resisted. A psychiatrist colleague described to me similar frustrations on interviewing prisoners for reports to court. He said that as he interviewed his 'therapeutic fingers itched'!

CLIENT ALLOCATION

Care taken in preliminary assessment has to be followed up by sensitive allocation of clients to counsellors. A client may have expressed a preference for one type of counsellor – one who has experienced a similar problem, an older counsellor, a woman or, less likely, a man. Practical considerations have to be taken into account – the client may only be able to attend at certain times. Some counsellors, especially in a small town, may be known to the client and therefore are inappropriate. Where home visits are made, distance may determine who is available. Sensitive allocation will take into account gender and racial issues.

At the same time the counselling co-ordinator has to bear in mind the interests of the counsellors. It is important that a trainee counsellor is given a range of clients. It may also be important in a generic agency that some counsellors develop a specialist interest, though not to the extent of preventing other counsellors from gaining a range of experience. Where allocation is in the hands of one person, it may be felt that some counsellors are favoured while others receive a constant succession of one-off attenders or no-hopers.

Cross-gender pairing in counselling can raise especially acute difficulties. In a companion volume on counselling and women's groups, Perry (1993) explores the power issues between the sexes which intrude into the counselling room and which deter some people from cross-gender pairings. Sexual feelings and exploitation are issues to be considered, the dangers of which are recognized in the unequivocal statement in the BAC's *Code of Ethics* that 'engaging in sexual activity with a client whilst also engaging in a therapeutic relationship is unethical' (BAC 1984: Section 2.7). There is a real danger that some male clients may be violent. Proper precautions need to be taken to ensure that women counsellors are happy to counsel men and that adequate security arrangements are in force.

The gender imbalance between the counsellor and client populations make a neat allocation impossible. Some people hold firm views that counselling across genders carries added benefits for some clients. This is a matter that needs further research. Counselling which focuses on issues such as parenting or sexual identity or intimate relationships must feel very different according to the gender of the counsellor. Allen's (1990: 24) sentiments cannot be unique: 'The only reason I went to the voluntary sector was to find a woman. All the private avenues I explored turned out to be men and I was not having one of them after the last time!'

Some clients specifically ask for a counsellor of the opposite gender. Those allocating cases then have a responsibility for closely examining the reasons. There may be danger signals. A request that is thought to be genuine, perhaps because of a history of failure to make relationships with the opposite sex, should be sympathetically considered. It should only be agreed if the counsellor, of whichever sex, feels safe about the assignment. A woman counsellor should not be left alone with a male client whom she has not had time to learn to trust. There should be someone else on hand in the building, or, if she is visiting the client's home, she should be accompanied by a colleague.

One counsellor was on her way to visit a new male client in a rural area after a briefing from the appointments secretary. She noticed as she drove through the village how deserted it was in the early afternoon. She found the house and the door was opened by a somewhat dishevelled man, considerably younger than she had anticipated. He waved her in to a room littered with empty bottles and cans, and slammed and locked the door behind her. She suddenly realized that she had not told anyone she was making this call. The appointments secretary knew of the client, of course, but not the day or time of the visit. Her family had only been told she would be out that afternoon. She was gripped by panic. However, she drew on all her wits and experience. She managed to get the client talking for some time, and she got out safely. Three days later she learned the client was admitted to hospital with a schizophrenic breakdown. This was not before she had promised her family and her colleagues that she would never again visit a client without someone knowing where she was going and for how long.

I do not want to be alarmist. Unpleasant incidents are fortunately rare. It is important for counselling agencies to create an accepting atmosphere and to trust people. It is also vital that staff in counselling offices are not put at risk. Those in walk-in agencies are particularly vulnerable to clients with mental health or addiction problems. Alarm buttons, emergency procedures known to all staff, and direct contact with a local police station are all sensible precautions. A management committee must be conscious of the need to exercise full responsibility for the safety of all its workers.

COLLEAGUE RELATIONSHIPS

Voluntary organizations not only have to recruit, train and care for their counsellors. Volunteers are needed to fill many other roles involving varied levels of commitment. They are needed to look after the office and act as receptionists, and sometimes to undertake practical tasks like driving the housebound. Some volunteers act as chaperones to counsellors seeing clients in a building on their own. Others work from home, taking phone calls from clients. The latter duty is a particularly onerous commitment, one which is sometimes helpfully taken on by someone confined to house or bed. Other occasional tasks occur which are greeted with varying degrees of enthusiasm – clearing the garden, decorating the premises, and running jumble sales, coffee mornings, gala concerts or street collections to raise funds.

This range of activities is one which starkly differentiates counselling in voluntary settings from professional counselling. Counsellors are expected to play their part in them. It can be irksome to the dedicated counsellors who can protest that cost-effectiveness lies in using their time in counselling rather than selling raffle tickets! The reality is that all these tasks are necessary. Hierarchical notions, understandable though they are, are not appropriate to the voluntary ethos. Yet there is still a tendency to elitism on the one side, and to envy and resentment on the other, springing from the disproportionate importance placed on the formation of counsellors.

All volunteers who are in touch in any way with the distress of clients should be carefully vetted for their roles, and all should receive the necessary support. In many voluntary agencies the telephones are answered by volunteers who on occasions find this extremely stressful. When asked what qualities were necessary for the such volunteers at Cruse branches, one response was 'a warm dressing gown'! This came from a branch which had not installed an answering machine. Its telephone may ring in the early hours of the morning, a time so dreaded by the grieving widow. The contact who answers the telephone knows it will be a long call. She knows that it is extremely unlikely that she can summon up any help from her branch colleagues at that hour. The caller may feel suicidal; the morning, and the offer of help then, may seem interminably far away. Alone, and without the back-up which is the hallmark of the Samaritans' service in such conditions, the contact listens and sympathizes and comforts as best she can, trusting as she hangs up that she has done something to ease the grief and give hope for tomorrow.

The volunteer in the office may be confronted with a similar situation when someone walks in unexpectedly. Such encounters are likely to happen in the best-resourced organizations and certainly in the bodies that rely heavily on a voluntary workforce. The volunteers can make a helpful response, even though feeling that they would be doing much better if they had had the benefit of counsellor training. What they need is someone to talk to about the encounter afterwards.

All these volunteers are part of a team. Like their counterparts in other settings, they have valuable parts to play in the therapeutic process. Like the ward cleaner, the school dinner lady, and other ancillary staff in institutions, receptionists and helpers in counselling offices play a part in providing care and attention to clients. Some clients find that a caring welcome by a receptionist with a spontaneous opportunity to talk about their troubles is all the help they require.

Counselling is by nature a very individual activity. Its hallmarks are privacy and confidentiality. It tends to attract as counsellors people who prefer working alone. Deliberate efforts have to be made to engender a corporate spirit and ensure that each person values the contribution of the other. This is particularly difficult in large groups where the counsellors may not all know each other, and in wide geographical areas where there may be several counselling outposts. Training events and social gatherings have a part to play in bringing people together.

The emotional commitment of volunteers to voluntary organizations can be strong and time-demanding. As these agencies provide opportunities for emotional growth and close personal involvement for the counsellors, spouses and partners can easily feel excluded, and they may resent the agency as the third party in their relationship! Some agencies try to bridge this gap by inviting partners to social events. Relate goes one step further by inviting the partners of new sex therapists to take part in the introductory weekend of training.

These offers are welcomed by some partners, but are not always taken up. They show a proper concern for the counsellors' relationships and are worth making. That, however, is the limit of the agency's responsibility. Counsellors themselves bear the responsibility for managing their own personal relationships.

The agency does carry responsibility for the professional and inter-agency relationships arising from the work. These are examined in the next chapter.

· FIVE ·

Professional relationships in counselling in the voluntary sector

INTERNAL RELATIONSHIPS

The strength of the voluntary counselling agencies traditionally lies in the one-to-one encounter between counsellor and client in the confidentiality of the counselling relationship. Counsellors are selected and trained to be agents of support and change for their clients. That is the *raison d'être* of the agencies. It is an activity which is highly person-centred. Administration tends to be seen as a necessary but secondary task which exists to provide the setting in which the counselling takes place. The services need good management to be used to their full effect.

This has parallels in other settings. Traditionally schools have been staffed almost entirely by teachers; the health service dominated by medical practitioners; and the railways were run for a long time by engineers. Now marketing men have taken over the running of the railways, hospital administrators manage the medical services and schools are struggling with the challenge of local management of schools.

Voluntary counselling services find themselves under similar pressures to strengthen their management structures. Increasingly their funding bodies scrutinize the way they manage their funds and their administration. In my own career I have lived through this shift in emphasis. When I became chief officer of NMGC in 1968, one of the reasons given for my appointment was that I was a practising counsellor. I left in 1986 when NMGC took the advice of management consultants that the post should be retitled and filled by a non-counsellor professional manager.

Management is gradually achieving a higher place in the priorities of voluntary organizations and their internal relationships. This is reflected, for instance, in the guidelines provided by Alcohol Concern to the counselling agencies in their network. The Volunteer Alcohol Counsellors Training Scheme (VACTS) has been produced by Alcohol Concern (1989) to promote good practice in all its county-based alcohol and drug counselling services and to set standards for assessing services. These guidelines give equal importance to standards of management and to standards of counselling. They encourage agencies to clarify their management structure and their philosophy. They lay down proposals of practice for involving volunteers. All this guidance is given in the belief that this will enable an agency 'to increase its flexibility, develop its staffing diversity and root itself fully into the community.' (Alcohol Concern 1992)

These guidelines are excellent. They include a contract setting out the responsibilities and amount of work expected of counsellors, and procedures relating to grievances, disciplinary matters, insurance and expenses. An equal opportunities policy is considered essential, under which there is monitoring of the degree to which all sections of the community are participating as staff, volunteers and clients. Advice is given about consultation with volunteers on aspects of agency policy and procedures.

The organizations associated with Alcohol Concern have the advantage of being almost entirely funded by local health authorities and central government project grants. They are able to pay their staff on local authority pay scales. This strengthens their hands in setting clear management guidelines. Such favourable conditions do not apply in many parts of the voluntary sector. In many of the agencies where funding is less assured, relationships between counsellors and administrators are not always easy. This can be particularly so where managers receive some payment and all the counsellors are volunteers. Counsellors can feel envious of the payment, and expect the administrator to do all the unpleasant tasks. The administrators can feel that they have the worst of all worlds, not having the kudos of working voluntarily, yet receiving a salary which is well below their real market value, often little more than an honorarium.

The appointment of a paid organizer for the first time can be a major step forward in the life cycle of a voluntary organization. The new post undoubtedly increases efficiency, but it has the effect of making a significant increase to the budget. It also significantly alters the balance of relationships in the agency. All too often the voluntary committee members react by lessening their personal involvement in the day-to-day running of affairs. The paid organizers can feel the weight of responsibility for everything, with their authority weakened by being a paid servant of the committee. There is also the added burden, either expressed or implied, that they should be able to increase income to meet the additional cost of their salaries. The lot of the only salaried staff member in a voluntary organization can be a lonely one.

Conscious efforts need to be taken to foster mutual understanding and goodwill. Occasional social gatherings are valuable in bringing together staff, committee members and volunteers who may not meet in the normal course of events. Opportunities need to be made for airing bad feelings and resentments, rather than allowing dissatisfactions to continue unexpressed and unresolved. In organizations which have a large number of volunteers, a formal system should be established for representatives of the various groups of volunteers to negotiate with the management. Conflicts are less likely to occur if clear definitions of roles and lines of management responsibility have been worked out, and if volunteers are aware of their obligations and their accountability.

A good management committee should be sensitive to any underlying currents and find ways of resolving them. Paid members of staff should be provided with a professional level of support and supervision. Such help is particularly important in places where there are only one or two staff who can easily become institutionalized and lose their objectivity. An agency which loses its sense of perspective and becomes caught up in factions and unresolved ill feelings quickly becomes a very unsafe place for young counsellors to exercise their newly acquired skills. A survey of counsellors who dropped out prematurely showed that such tensions featured high in the reasons given by newcomers for early resignation (Heisler 1974).

INTER-AGENCY PARTNERSHIP

Collaboration between agencies can also receive low priority in the voluntary sector. In practice, collaboration is costly in terms of time and personnel. With resources so often stretched, it may seem that the effort to get co-operation between agencies far outweighs the benefits which are gained by it.

Formal structures exist for bringing voluntary organizations together, such as the National Council of Voluntary Child Care Organisations, Charity Forum and the National Council for Voluntary

Organisations. At national level these aim to stimulate cross-fertilization of ideas and practice, and disseminate information across relevant parts of the voluntary sector. These laudable objectives can be achieved, but only if organizational representatives are prepared to commit themselves to frequent meetings. The benefits accrue mostly in long-term planning and development. For agencies burdened in the present with constant pressure from clients which they cannot meet, such activities are often considered an unaffordable luxury.

At a local level, meetings of the equivalent bodies can be of more immediate use. In most localities, the number of key people in organizations of this sort is small enough to enable them to get on personal terms. They have greater potential for developing trustworthy relationships. Inevitably there is some rivalry and competition, since the organizations all solicit the same local companies and trusts for support, and seek to recruit from the same pool of potential voluntary workers. Where good community spirit exists these natural rivalries can be tolerated. Many voluntary organizations find that they thrive in small or medium-sized towns, even where there is a plethora of voluntary agencies. It is much more difficult to capitalize on community spirit in a large conurbation. It is particularly hard to maintain thriving community bodies with voluntary counsellors in the large London boroughs. Big is not beautiful.

Voluntary agencies that perceive themselves to be equal partners can achieve a working relationship with each other. Relations between voluntary organizations and local authorities are more complicated. One study has emphasized that feelings of equality are often lacking:

> The understanding of partnership as a collaborative relationship between local authorities and local voluntary organizations through which each carries a joint responsibility for planning, policy making and implementation as part of a whole, and where voluntary organizations enjoy parity of status and influence, is one that exists more in theory than reality.
>
> (Brenton 1985: 128)

This study concludes that the relationship is too unequal to be a partnership. Furthermore, the prognosis is a gloomy one. This inequality can only increase in the current political climate, as voluntary agencies come under increasing external pressures that seem designed to manipulate them into becoming the privatized sector of the social services.

A further blockage to inter-agency collaboration is located by

Woodhouse and Pengelly (1991) within the unconscious anxieties and defence mechanisms of the services themselves. The authors are professional caseworkers from the Tavistock Institute. They report on an inter-disciplinary study programme, in which they worked for three years with voluntary marriage counsellors, general practitioners, social workers, probation officers and health visitors. The authors were struck by the difficulties of collaboration, even between practitioners from the same area who had a unique opportunity of sustaining close colleague relationships in the project over this extended period.

They commented on the pressures felt by the workers in the study arising from their experience of working at an intimate level with clients on their pain and loss. These pressures unconsciously cause practitioners to use the structures and boundaries of their agencies as a defence against collaboration (Woodhouse and Pengelly 1991: 228). It was significant that confidentiality was generally claimed as the reason for not working together on behalf of clients. The authors point out that the validity of that claim was seldom tested by efforts to achieve a realistic balance between confidentiality and co-operation among equal fellow practitioners.

The group in that project which appeared to be least able to form collaborative relationships outside their own discipline was the counsellors (Woodhouse and Pengelly 1991: 69). They suffered from the handicap of being the only participants in the study programme who were working voluntarily. However, they had the advantage of being the most experienced group on the topic of the programme, which was marital relations. This suggests that a lack of collaboration is particularly liable to occur where counsellors are involved. This may be because counselling is in essence about privacy and intimacy. Or perhaps it is because counselling attracts as practitioners individuals who prefer solitary work settings and do not readily want to mix with others.

The stark conclusion of the study is that inter-agency collaboration throughout the caring professions only becomes possible when each agency is fully confident in its own work. Good relationships require accurate knowledge of each other, mutual trust and confidence. If these are lacking, referral of clients between agencies is often inappropriate. Woodhouse and Pengelly consider that many referrals are hasty and ill-thought out. Consciously or unconsciously, practitioners use referrals as a way of getting rid of clients they are not able to help rather than as a genuinely positive means of help. They conclude that referrals constitute 'the point of maximum dishonesty'. (1991: 67)

Dishonesty of a different sort lies in hanging on to clients too long. All agencies should be able to assess when they are not the ones best placed to help a particular client. They need to have sufficient knowledge of the counselling network to inform the client where more appropriate help is available. Each counsellor should conscientiously be considering whether additional or alternative help would be right for a client.

There are temptations to continue too long with a client. A counsellor may either be ignorant of alternative sources of help, or may attach an exaggeratedly high importance to the strength of the therapeutic alliance with that client. These are issues which have to be weighed up carefully. Referrals are sometimes helpful, but not if the belief that another agency is able to provide more effective relief for a client's problems is based more on wishful thinking than on reality.

These pessimistic conclusions need not cause voluntary agencies to abandon efforts at collaboration. The clear message from Woodhouse and Pengelly is that effective co-operation can only be achieved if the difficulties in inter-agency relationships are fully addressed. Collaboration is important for serving the best interests of clients and practitioners. The helping network needs to be sufficiently understood to be of use as a means of identifying the most appropriate help for clients. It is easy to play at collaboration. In that way the network can be abused. Clients can be passed round from agency to agency as if they were unwanted parcels. Such practice is not helpful for agencies or client. It may be used as a way of disguising the unpalatable fact that, for some clients, no appropriate help is available.

THE CONTRIBUTION OF PROFESSIONALS

Members of the helping professions have played a major role in establishing many of the voluntary agencies. Social workers, doctors, lawyers, psychologists and ministers of religion have been the driving force in many of them. In particular, we have seen how voluntary counselling at the outset learned from, and was generously encouraged by, psychiatrists with an analytic orientation.

The voluntary sector is keen to retain the involvement of people from the professions in many ways. Often this takes the form of active membership of a management committee, or contributing expert assistance with training or supervision. It may be little more than nominal support, either as consultants whose specialist advice can be called on occasionally, or as prestigious patrons appearing on the notepaper, giving credibility to the organization. The annual reports of some of the early national counselling organizations contained long lists of names, categorized under such headings as medical, legal, spiritual and psychiatric advisory boards. The boards never assembled but they demonstrated professional recognition for the young agencies.

Advisory boards of a more active kind now exist in some places. They are a creative way of maintaining inter-professional partnership. The boards bring together those responsible within the agency for counselling, training and research with interested professionals on the periphery with relevant expertise. There may be about a dozen members, few enough to work as a group yet allowing for diversity of representation from different disciplines. Meetings take place two or three times a year to review aspects of agency practice and generate new ideas. The mode of working is more akin to a think tank than a structured committee meeting. Experts from other bodies or people visiting from overseas can be invited to make presentations from time to time. Such a broad forum can be a sounding board for examining internal plans, and can play a major role in countering an inward-looking attitude (Lewis *et al.* 1992: 153). For the professionals involved it can be an effective use of their expert knowledge, which can be percolated more widely through volunteers.

In-house research is another potential field for an advisory board. Research generally features as one of the officially stated Objects of any counselling organization which is a charity, but it is often vulnerable to pressures of time or money, and is lacking in most agencies. In the 1970s, when NMGC had a quarterly journal, annual research seminars, a full-time research officer and published a series of research monographs, I wrote:

> Research is not easy to undertake in voluntary social service organisations. Finance is never adequate, demands are enormous, and research tends to slip down the list of priorities in face of the pressure to maintain the service. However the service can rapidly become sterile unless it is constantly monitored.
>
> (Lewis *et al.* 1992: 264)

These words were unfortunately prophetic. All research projects and publications in that agency have since been disbanded.

While it existed, the NMGC Research Advisory Board consisted of research workers from universities and institutes involved in marital research. It advised on the initiatives to be taken with in-house monitoring and dissemination of results. It hosted a regular forum for field workers. From that there developed meetings of counsellors, trainers and researchers to explore the problems which impede partnership between these three groups, and examine why research results rarely lead to action upon them. The aim was to increase mutual understanding, to lessen the marginalization of the researchers and to stimulate research-mindedness in counsellors themselves.

At a local level, similar benefits derive from contributions of various kinds from professionals. They willingly give specialist input to local organizations whose aims they support, but it is important to make best use of their time and expertise. Busy psychiatrists, with the best will in the world, soon begin to doubt the value of time spent at executive committees whose agendas consist of business matters with which they are unfamiliar. They can, however, make a valuable contribution to a sub-committee concerned with technical matters or assessment of counsellors, or to a working party reviewing and planning training. Genuine partnership must be grounded in recognition and use of the individual talents of each member.

FUNDING BODIES

'Partnership' is a word increasingly used in the voluntary sector in relation to funding bodies. In their initial stages, most agencies seek funds in many and varied ways. Appeals are made to local bodies such as Rotary, Round Table and the Soroptimists, churches, businesses and local trusts. Fund-raising events are held, from coffee mornings and concerts to bazaars and lotteries. Individual subscriptions may be sought. With an enthusiastic fund-raising group and a well-presented case, adequate early support is generally forthcoming.

As work extends and the budget grows, it becomes necessary to put income on a more stable basis. *Ad hoc* fund-raising efforts on their own are too unpredictable to underpin substantial worthwhile activity. Most agencies would do well to heed Brenton's (1985: 221) advice to 'continue to solicit their funds from a variety of sources if they value their separate identity and autonomy, and are to avoid dependence and incorporation'. This entails seeking core funding from both statutory and private sources that are prepared to provide a significant proportion of the fixed costs.

Fund-raising activities are essential in themselves to ensure income. For many voluntary organizations they also fulfil the secondary objective of informing the community about their presence and work. Appeals to influential individuals and corporate groups in the community serve as an important educational medium.

Some agencies are funded substantially from public funds and do not have to engage in extensive fund-raising activities. They can concentrate their efforts on service provision. The Department of Health's drug prevention and education programme funds many of the addiction agencies. Victim Support gets 75% of its funding from the Home Office through the crime prevention budget. The Women's Royal Voluntary Service, which gives very practical help to the housebound, although not a counselling organization, receives 100% Home Office funding for its core activities. Many mental health counselling agencies, such as Open Door and those being pioneered under the auspices of MIND, are funded through Care in the Community grants. Where public funds form all or most of an agency's income, the agency is relieved of day-to-day money worries. It has to submit a case for renewed funding annually or triennially, and it is circumscribed in its activities accordingly. The danger is, of course, that the agency is more vulnerable to government cuts than one that has many different sources of income.

Central government also has a history of part-funding voluntary bodies. As a move to rationalize this burgeoning level of financial support, the Home Office set up the Voluntary Services Unit in 1974. The Unit served as a co-ordinating body across all departments of government. Its grants were crucial in supporting a wide range of services provided at that time in the voluntary sector. The main concept of this funding was to provide the core costs of organizations which satisfied the government that they were providing necessary and competent services. That enabled the organizations to continue with their basic work with a sense of security, while looking for other sources of income to fund development. New projects therefore depended on attracting additional non-statutory contributions. This was a satisfactory arrangement for the voluntary bodies, as experience shows that private funds can most easily be obtained for new ventures where the donors are happy to play a pump-priming role. Private donors and trustees are not keen to contribute to regular administrative costs that show no specific outcome.

Recent policy in government departments appears to be departing from this established practice. There is growing reluctance on the part of government to provide continuous grants to meet the core funding of established voluntary organizations. Government grants are increasingly being confined to new projects, and they are time-limited. This is a worrying trend for voluntary bodies who have to maintain their central administrative structures. It comes at a time when the voluntary sector is already under threat in other ways. Currently recession is endangering private contributions to an alarming degree. At the same time, more bodies, from hospital trusts to universities and museums, are trawling for private funding from the sources which have traditionally supported voluntary social service, so competition is fierce. Those voluntary organizations which have traditionally depended on government for core funding can no longer do so.

For local organizations the picture is more varied. Agencies apply to local government authorities and to health service authorities at all levels. The response differs markedly, and randomly. Branches of the same national body in different parts of the country receive widely differing grants. Some authorities are generous in support, not only with money but also with various forms of material help. For instance, many health authorities assist with training of volunteers by allowing their training centres, with all their facilities, to be used without payment, and encouraging their staff to participate. Many local authorities have a tradition of providing rent-free office premises for some voluntary bodies.

Relationships with these statutory bodies have to be nurtured. It is worth expending time and effort to submit applications annually to all tiers of local and health authorities. It is important to establish personal links with key individuals on those authorities, both elected representatives and paid staff. Bodies that give grants have a right to know how their money is spent. But it is equally important to have someone on those bodies with an informed interest in the counselling service. All statutory bodies get many applications. The decision to approve one of them may be strongly influenced by someone in the authority who can speak with personal knowledge of the worth of the agency. The professionalism of the service can be communicated in all sorts of ways – co-opting a borough councillor on to the management committee, inviting the director of social services to speak at a public meeting, or even arranging a photocall for the mayor to cut the cake at a significant anniversary celebration.

Like many other supplicants, the voluntary counselling agencies are having to seek new ways of attracting money from industry and trusts. Warnings have been sounded concerning this new trend. Butler and Wilson (1990: 168) point out that 'recent developments by some charities to try to secure additional funding from commercial organisations run the risk of inflexibility by increasing their dependence'. However, it is a path that counselling agencies must follow along with the other agencies and institutions.

The time-honoured practice for voluntary organizations of receiving a large percentage of their income in grants without strings from philanthropic bodies is slowly changing. The emphasis is increasingly on establishing partnerships with funding bodies which put the onus on the voluntary agency to provide some specific return for financial assistance. This takes several forms. It may entail acknowledging in annual reports or publicity brochures that sponsorship for the publication has been provided by named companies. A new service, such as a telephone advice line, may need to be advertised with the name of the firm who funded it. It may mean giving priority for counselling to employees of a sponsoring body. It may involve agreeing a contract with a donor firm to provide counselling for its staff over retirement or redundancy, or run courses for the staff on human relations skills.

This kind of partnership may raise ethical issues. At best it is a relationship which results in improved services for clients and extra publicity for the sponsoring body. But, where 'he who pays the piper calls the tune', uncomfortable dilemmas arise for the voluntary agencies. The agency may come to be overidentified in the public mind with one particular product or firm. The association may be especially unfortunate if the company receives criticism because it trades in products which come under criticism on health, environmental or political grounds. Then there is the disadvantage that priority for clients from one source is likely to mean longer waiting lists for other groups of clients. And financial considerations rather than professional ones can come to determine staff deployment and allocation of clients, with the normal basic service for clients suffering accordingly.

As far as the agencies themselves are concerned, the positive side of sponsorship is that it gives security through provision of a guaranteed level of income, at least for the negotiated period. In contrast, substantial one-off payments, welcome though they are, provide no such stability. Windfalls can have the effect of overinflating short-term income, and giving the impression to potential funders that their donations are not needed. Wise treasurers record bequests or donations of that magnitude under a separate heading, perhaps opening a development fund, in order not to distort the annual income/expenditure balance sheet. The money can then be earmarked for extraordinary items of expenditure rather than being absorbed into general running costs.

Once voluntary organizations have established themselves and their existence is assured, it is important that they estimate their financial requirements two, three or five years ahead. This demands a fundamental change from the *ad hoc* funding which characterizes the early years of most bodies. Financial expertise has to be acquired, in the first instance generally in the form of an honorary treasurer. Bank officials are in great demand for this task. They are able to institute adequate financial controls. However, a stage is reached when financial planning is needed. This is much more than accurate book-keeping. An overcautious treasurer can impede development. Risks must sometimes be taken. Voluntary bodies need to find a financial controller who understands the dangers of going into the red but is sufficiently committed to the mission of the agency to balance that risk against the imperative of developing the service. Finance has to become a creative tool of management rather than a dead hand.

Once established, there is also the danger that too much will be expected of the voluntary services. Butler and Wilson (1990: 170) offer another warning. 'The role of the voluntary sector is in process of becoming more a stand-alone provider of services rather than an adjunct to those provided by the state.' Certainly, growing demands are being made on the voluntary sector as a by-product of government policies such as the emptying of long-stay psychiatric hospitals and the provision of non-custodial treatment schemes for offenders. Desirable though these policies are, they increase the number of people seeking help and the complexity of issues they bring. They impose particular pressure on mental health agencies such as the counselling services. Government departments have not increased their grants to voluntary bodies in proportion to these extra demands.

This lays the government open to the charge that it is treating the voluntary sector as a cheap option. In so doing, it is exploiting the goodwill of volunteers, and is in danger of putting a greater load on the voluntary sector than it can bear. Consequences can be dire. Management committees then expect miracles from their paid staff, and members become angry and disillusioned when these are not forthcoming. Relationships in the organizations, and standards of service, suffer accordingly.

ETHICS AND VALUES

Along with funding issues for voluntary organizations, it is vital to present an acceptable image to the public. It must be accurate and informative, but it should also catch the imagination of the public.

This can be a source of conflict between different groups within the agencies.

The responsibility for public relations is often given to a sub-group of the management committee. The group may be keen to present the agency to the outside world in immediate and dramatic terms. Public relations officers in agencies know that good media copy rests on firm claims, sensational stories and measurable results. They want black and white statements and eye-catching headlines. However, those counselling in the agency know that their counselling is often far from dramatic and immediate. Their emphasis may be to discourage their clients from hoping for quick remedies, to help them to sort out their problems sensitively but slowly. They may be reluctant to make optimistic claims about success rates.

This dilemma can be seen clearly in the children's societies. Their fund-raising appeal lies in stories of children who are victims of violence or sexual assault. They need to publish authentic reports accompanied, if possible, by pictures of bruised and frightened children. The social workers in the societies working with the children and their families have a very different view of their task. They aspire to work with the whole family. They know how important it is to keep the confidence of these families. 'Shock horror' publicity not only gives a false impression of their aims, but also may undermine their clientele's belief that the agency is a neutral confidential place where families having difficulties with their children can safely refer themselves. The public relations officer is keen to hear sensational stories on which to base publicity for gaining support from the community, but can find that efforts to elicit real live case material are frustrated by the social workers.

Marital agencies face internal conflicts of a different sort. These agencies enjoy substantial funding from the Home Office. This is negotiated on grounds that marital counselling is less costly than the divorce process, and is therefore a saving to the public purse. The official line of the agencies still talks in terms of marriages that are kept together through counselling. However, their counsellors adopt a more neutral stance. For them, a successful outcome is not necessarily one that results in a couple staying together. It may equally lie in improved communication or in resolution of painful problems, whether cohabitation continues or not. A separation which is amicably agreed by both partners as the best thing for the family is as much a success as a resumed marital relationship. A recent chronicler of marriage guidance views this as a continuing dilemma. 'Relate's ideas, purpose and mission were as vulnerable to political as to financial pressures in the 1980s' (Lewis *et al.* 1992: 200). She adds significantly that 'it proved difficult to acknowledge and discuss the conflicting pressures'.

Conflicts likewise exist in denominational agencies, where objectives and values may be open to different interpretations. The Jewish Marriage Council, for instance, opens its counselling service to all Jews, but the Council itself is based in a strict orthodox tradition. Its function at the outset was to provide marriage preparation courses to ensure that young couples were instructed in the rites and customs of traditional Jewish marriages. Among other services, it operates a marriage bureau for bringing orthodox young people together, with the aim of maintaining Jewish family traditions. Its counsellors, however, find themselves working with mixed marriages and with couples who are at odds with the traditional Jewish way of life and are seeking to break away from it. They have to maintain a balancing act of loyalty to their own traditions while helping clients tease out their own cultural and domestic solutions.

These denominational issues are explored more fully in Lyall's (1995) volume in this series. They are important to other agencies who may wish to refer clients with specifically spiritual problems, but are suspicious about the implications of a denominational label. The word 'Christian' appearing in the title of an organization carries very variable connotations. At one extreme it may indicate an approach which is closer to evangelism than to the psychological counselling which is the concern of this book. Such 'Christian counsellors' have a training based on Bible study which leads them to look to the Scriptures for the answer to the personal dilemmas of their clients. Prayer, exposition and exhortation are likely to feature largely in their counselling. It is unlikely such agencies will be used by professionals for making referrals.

Confidence can be placed in some other counselling agencies in Christian contexts. They cater for clients who seek psychological help but want it in the security of a setting where counsellor and client have a shared religious commitment. The nature of such commitment is more likely to be a mutual awareness of the importance of a spiritual dimension to life than adherence to a specific church or dogma. In the words of the Westminster Pastoral Foundation, which had its origins in the Methodist Church but is not now a religious organization in the conventional sense, its centres 'seek to combine a concern for spiritual values and meanings as essential aspects of human living, with the professional practice of the disciplines of psychotherapy and counselling'.

Counsellors need to deal sensitively with spiritual topics whatever agency they work in. In some Christian organizations the use of prayer, spiritual guidance, healing and laying on of hands, confession and absolution may be valid parts of counselling with some clients (Jacobs 1983: Chapter 10). In non-denominational agencies counsellors may feel less confident in handling specifically religious matters when a client raises them. Yet it is essential that a counsellor working with a client after a bereavement should be confident enough to explore matters of belief about death and after-life. Quite frequently clients at such a point want to talk about whether to become involved with spiritualism or visit mediums. It is as inappropriate to deprive individual clients of the opportunity of exploring life and death understandings at the time of bereavement as it is to thrust some uninvited dogma on them.

Within any team of counsellors in the voluntary sector there are likely to be different perspectives on spiritual and religious issues. Some counsellors are more open to exploring them and handle them more confidently than others. Caution in such matters is wise, and the advice might be noted that 'the pastoral counsellor needs to use his or her religious base sparingly and implicitly, and only to address religious issues explicitly if and when these are introduced by the client' (Foskett and Jacobs 1991: 255).

It is important that the counselling relationship is kept free of specific dogmatic pressure. It is also important that the belief and value systems of agencies are made explicit, so that referrers and clients are clear about what are the implications of any denominational title. Professionals considering referring their clients for counselling are likely to fight shy of any agency they suspect of evangelistic intentions.

CLIENT REFERRALS

The most frequent occasions for counselling agencies to have contact with other agencies and professions is over client referrals. In voluntary organizations clients generally refer themselves. Effective counselling requires a high degree of motivation, which involves both keeping appointments and co-operating with the process of working to gain insight or to solve personal problems. The experience of some agencies is that clients who are referred by third parties, such as relatives or professional workers, are less likely to commit themselves to the possibility of change through counselling.

The onus is therefore placed on clients themselves to make appointments and to keep or cancel them; and to communicate back, if they wish, to anyone who encouraged them to refer themselves. In practice, this means that people who telephone on behalf of someone they are working with professionally are generally asked to encourage that person to make his or her own appointment. Where the agency has a close professional relationship with the referrer, it may accept the referrer's assurance that the client is fully aware of the request. But it is preferable for the client to make the first request personally. The same goes for anyone calling with concern about a friend or relative.

Such calls require careful handling because they must not imply that the caller's concern is misplaced. A skilled response to this sort of call not only explains the reason for such a procedure but also acknowledges the care the caller has taken. The outcome of the call may be different than anticipated. During discussion of the problem it may become apparent that the worker telephoning is handling the issue satisfactorily, and only needs assurance to carry on with the client. With family and friends also, it may seem that the informal carers are giving as appropriate help as possible. A worried aunt, for instance, who telephoned to ask a counsellor to visit her nephew, ended the call by realizing that she was the person best placed to talk with the boy, and with a better understanding of how to go about it.

A referral system has to take into account not only the best interests of the client but also relationships between the agency and those who want to make referrals to it. To foster good inter-agency understanding, some agencies, with the consent of the client, send a letter informing the referring professional that a client has been accepted for counselling. Such letters rarely invite close collaboration between the helpers involved. It is preferable that clients are encouraged themselves to inform the person who referred them that they are receiving counselling, and to give them any feedback about it that is appropriate. This especially applies to referrals from general practitioners.

If clients fail to keep appointments, some agencies make a point of writing to offer another appointment. Appointments secretaries have to exercise discretion because there are many reasons for a failure to turn up for a first appointment. It may be cold feet at the last minute ('the car wouldn't start' is a frequent cry), or a dramatic change in the personal situation since, and possibly because of, making the first appointment. Experience in NMGC shows that an average of 18% of first appointments are not kept. Local centres accept such a failure rate as the norm. If the percentage goes much higher they need to examine their procedures for responding to initial calls, to see if any alterations need to be made.

Agencies have their own policies about what action to take when clients who have already started counselling miss appointments. Generally it is the counsellor who decides on what action to take. An unkept appointment may be a client's way of testing out the counsellor's commitment. The counsellor may decide not to follow it up, but to remain available for a week or two in case the client makes a new approach. Some agencies encourage counsellors to send a letter noting the unkept appointment and offering a new one. Circumstances vary greatly, and any response or decision not to respond should be thought out in response to the individual situation. Much depends on the degree of trust already established between counsellor and client. In so far as counselling is concerned to value individuals whose self-esteem is often low, it is best to err on the side of acknowledging an unkept appointment, rather than being thought by the client to be lacking in care and concern.

Sometimes counselling agencies are criticized for not being more communicative to third parties about their work with individual clients. Doctors and other professionals who refer clients may be naturally curious about how counselling is progressing. In the nature of counselling, however, it is right and proper that control over communications about clients lies in the hands of the clients themselves. Agencies need to ensure this. There is also a practical reason for such minimal communication. The offices of most voluntary counselling services lack sufficient secretarial facilities for counsellors to use. In the voluntary sector, therefore, counsellors are unlikely to enter into correspondence in other than exceptional circumstances. Where there is a paid counselling organizer in post, opportunities for general communication about clients may be made, especially where there is a need to foster inter-agency co-operation.

Communications with doctors pose special issues for counsellors. Each client they meet is already the patient of a doctor. In many agencies it is doctors who refer the highest percentage of clients for counselling. Whereas the working relationship between counsellor and client is time-limited, that between doctor and patient is continuing. A counsellor is unlikely to see a client again once the crisis or particular difficulty has been resolved. A doctor's responsibility does not finish when one set of consultations with a patient comes to an end. Doctor and patient meet up again on later occasions.

Counselling agencies are aware of these special factors. Many make a point of recording the name of the client's doctors in case of emergency, though that information is acted on infrequently. As was discussed earlier in this chapter, professional ambivalence can complicate relationships between counsellors and doctors.

Counselling bodies have been spurred by such considerations to take initiatives in making closer links with the medical profession. In the 1970s voluntary counsellors in small numbers began to do counselling sessions in doctors' surgeries. The pioneer projects reported an uneasy and unequal relationship between doctors and counsellors (Marsh and Barr 1975; Heisler 1979; Wyld 1981). Voluntary counsellors have now gained more confidence of working in health settings, and the medical staff have learnt to value their specialist contribution. In some places reciprocal arrangements occur, with doctors advising counsellors on medical aspects of their clients' problems. Gradually the confidence of the medical profession in counselling increased, and counsellors began to see themselves, and perform, as members of health care teams. This provides the best setting for those clients who benefit most from simultaneously receiving talk therapy and medication. The counsellors and doctors also benefit, as it is in these circumstances that closer collaboration is achieved (Woodhouse and Pengelly 1991: 69), even though the counsellors are seen as auxiliaries. The special aspects of counselling in these settings will be explored more fully in a companion volume in this series (East 1995).

Though development of counselling in specialist medical settings has undoubtedly had beneficial effects, the dilemma of interdisciplinary relationships still remains in the non-medical settings where the vast majority of counselling takes place. A tripartite partnership of counsellor, doctor and patient/client would often be sensible. But co-operation on behalf of clients rarely manages to cross the professional divide when the practitioners are working in two different places.

Some counsellors and agencies expect their clients to have an exclusive relationship with them. They look with suspicion on clients who are receiving concurrent help elsewhere. They ask for an undivided commitment to counselling with them. This is particularly likely in any agency which undertakes long-term counselling. A less purist approach values the possibility of extra help from the use of two or more sources at the same time, as long as there does not appear to be evidence of splitting by the client, in the form of conscious or unconscious attempts to play off one practitioner against another. Examples of use of different resources include clients who are undergoing counselling for some emotional issue, and simultaneously are consulting a priest for spiritual guidance, or a doctor for attention to their symptoms of stress.

Counsellors and their supervisors need to bear in mind the possibility, and advisability at times, of encouraging clients to seek other forms of assistance. This might mean gaining legal or financial information from a solicitor, debt counsellor or Citizens' Advice Bureau. In grief counselling this might involve enquiring at a hospital for records of disposal after stillbirth, or, with adopted clients, searching for their natural families. Clients in danger of becoming overdependent on counselling might need firm encouragement to find additional social or quasi-therapeutic support elsewhere. With clients who are presenting with what may be thought of as psychosomatic symptoms, it may be necessary at some stage to suggest a medical examination to check that there is no physical cause.

Though these comments may seem to point to the obvious, counselling does contain traps for the unwary. It is important that counsellors do not get so caught up with emotional issues that they ignore simple practical matters, and the anxiety that such matters can generate in clients. It is negligent to continue treating as an emotional issue something that has an underlying physical cause. Nevertheless, a balance has to be kept between taking practical action too precipitously and completely ignoring the need for it.

Many of these forms of help or other opinions can be sought alongside a continuing counselling relationship. Referral or advice to get information elsewhere does not mean ending the counselling relationship. Counsellors should offer to go on meeting with clients, not least to talk through the outcome of any actions that arise from seeking other forms of help. Clients can be encouraged to seek medical advice, or have an AIDS/IIIV test, or search out the records of their family of origin, or apply to a dating agency, or negotiate with the debt retrieval company, and invited to return afterwards to discuss the implications. This invitation by the counsellor shows that referral elsewhere is not a dismissal or rejection. It is an assurance that the emotional issues accompanying practical factors are still being given their proper weight.

The best counselling offices keep up-to-date information on all relevant services in their locality. This is of use for pointing inappropriate referrals in the right direction. It also benefits counsellors by keeping them aware of the range of alternative services that are available. This chapter has explored professional relationships in the voluntary counselling agencies. There really is a danger that the wealth of these external sources of help may be overlooked in the intensity of relationships in the counselling room. A constant struggle for all counsellors is to preserve the value and uniqueness of their relationships with their clients, but at the same time not lose sight of the external world and its complementary resources.

SIX

A critique of counselling in the voluntary sector

ASPIRATIONS AND CONSTRAINTS

A circular from the Community Health Council had asked for comments from voluntary organizations about the provision of psychological and counselling help for patients who had had an abortion following rape or incest. The request was being considered by the counselling sub-committee in a local voluntary agency. Differing views were expressed. The psychiatric adviser was clear that such work required skilled professional intervention and that the training provided by the agency did not fit the counsellors to undertake it. The training officer demurred and thought at least that patients should be told of the availability of the service, and that a counsellor experienced in loss and victim trauma could be assigned should such a client ask for help at any time after her discharge from hospital. The counsellor representative suggested that the service should be advertised to the patient's family and friends, who might have been upset by the events and whose needs might not be met by the hospital. The organizer feared that such publicity would imply that the agency would take all such cases and would overtax the present team of counsellors.

This discussion encapsulates some of the main dilemmas in voluntary counselling agencies. What problems is the agency competent to tackle? What quality of service should be provided? How much counselling can be made available? What risks can be taken responsibly? When should further expansion and development be resisted?

Good management continually addresses these questions, and

balances the conflicting viewpoints and claims which are inevitable within any organization. Most counselling agencies do not have a formal voice representing the users of the service, so it is essential in this balancing act to ensure that the needs of clients and potential clients are kept to the fore. It is all too easy, in the pressure of maintaining all the different parts of the agency, to make it appear that the maxim is 'clients come last'.

Voluntary counselling agencies comprise a network of social concern. In this book I have interpreted the term 'counselling' widely, using it to mean the response made by the personal services in the voluntary sector to people in need. This may be formally organized individual counselling, similar to psychotherapy. It may be counselling families or groups. It may be the means through which a specific service is given, such as happens with the burgeoning demands on workers in Citizens' Advice Bureaux to provide debt counselling. There they have to use a counselling approach in examining with clients their income and expenditure, and planning ways of meeting financial commitments. Counselling may be available through informal contacts during occupational therapy or social group work, or through self-help and mutual aid groups. It may demand a proactive challenging mode, as with much counselling in addiction. It may entail help of a more reactive kind, as with clients suffering loss through crime or death. It may be a one-off session. It may be continuous sessions of counselling over months.

This network of social concern is complementary to the informal network of family and friends which has been the traditional means of providing social support to people in crisis. The informal network still functions adequately within some groups and cultures. This traditional support has been weakened in many sub-groups, however, because of social and economic changes – smaller families, greater mobility, an ageing population, increasingly complicated family relationships following divorce and remarriage, higher rates of unemployment, expectations of increased quality of life, often frustrated through unforeseen economic hazards, and disintegration of a shared system of religious belief.

Faced with the weakening of this informal network, the state is increasingly drawn into taking over from families some of their responsibilities for individual care. It now largely provides the formal support network through education, social services and medical care, though there are growing gaps in social provision. The voluntary sector has developed as a third force to fill these gaps. The official formal services provided by the state, and the informal support system of family and neighbourhood, continue to function.

The voluntary social service network exists alongside, linking and complementing the other two.

The voluntary sector enjoys a freedom from ties and controls; but this freedom makes it vulnerable to excessive demands, especially at a time when the state is engaged on making savage cuts in its services. The voluntary agencies experience contradictory pulls. They want to retain the warmth, spontaneity and initiative of good family and neighbourhood networks, which, in the best traditional sense, give support to those in distress. At the same time they aspire to the standards and structures of the statutory bodies in the formal network, despite lacking the resources formerly available to those services.

The growth of the voluntary counselling network in the last quarter of the twentieth century has been dramatic but uneven. It is mainly provided through specialist agencies which exist to deal with specific conditions or problems. The *Best Counselling Guide* (Quilliam and Gore-Stephensen 1991) identifies 27 'issues' under which counselling agencies are grouped. Virtually all these groups are comprised of voluntary bodies. The issues include eating disorders, phobias and depression; alcoholism, drug dependency and smoking; gay or lesbian relationships; handicaps or disabilities; religion, sexuality, suicide and bereavement; couples counselling, family therapy and culturally based counselling.

IDENTIFYING GAPS

In spite of this plethora of agencies, new gaps continue to be identified and new services established. Schizophrenia has for long been a very common and distressing complaint, yet there was no specific counselling service for sufferers and their families until 1992 when SANE (Schizophrenia – A National Emergency) opened a telephone helpline to provide a support and advisory service for people involved in any way with the illness.

There is still a scarcity of services for men. Gay Bereavement and other homosexual groups deal mainly with men. But there are few specialist points of reference, for instance, for males who are victims of domestic violence or sexual abuse. They are free to approach the generic services, but some men are reluctant to go there, fearing they are too female-orientated. Self-help groups for men are also rare. The ones that flourish, such as Families Need Fathers, are motivated by a strong sense of injustice arising, for instance, from judgements made in domestic courts about custody of children.

There is, as yet, no general tradition of men establishing their own counselling services.

As many of the agencies are problem-specific, there is still a gap where people are suffering from a condition which has not been identified or named. When myalgic encephalomyelitis (ME) was discovered sufferers reported experiencing enormous relief that their condition was finally recognized (Mayne 1987). Until it had been classified and labelled, no one knew how to respond to them. Doctors and counsellors were at a loss whether to offer drugs or talk therapy, and sufferers were left unsure if they were ill or merely malingering. Once the condition was named, the ME Association was soon formed and built up a body of understanding on which mutual support and counselling could be provided.

No such support yet exists for one family I knew whose child was confined to a wheelchair with a form of paralysis which has no known cause or name. Generic services were available and dealt helpfully with other forms of paralysis. But it was the unknown nature of this particular illness which was at the heart of this family's distress. They had no reference point for meeting with professionals or other sufferers who could help them with these 'unknowns'. Faced with this lack, this family considered taking its own initiative to contact families in a similar position for mutual support. A new gap had been identified and would thus receive attention.

One way of viewing the voluntary counselling sector is to see it as a progression from small spontaneous beginnings to professionally competent agencies offering a specific counselling service. Most of these beginnings have few resources and little experience to guide them. Occasionally the inspiration comes from someone who has experience elsewhere. But for small independent bodies there is no external help available as exists in the statutory social services – no network of journals and conferences for small counselling businesses. Where groups wish to establish a new branch of one of the existing national networks, help is forthcoming in the form of a starter guidance pack and advice from an area manager. But independent bodies have to set out anew to reinvent the wheel.

I became involved in one such potential beginning when I moved to a small town where a handful of members of the churches had attended a counselling course some miles away. They asked me to run a support group for them. At this stage they had no specific roles or structure, indeed they had no common view about their aspirations, merely a shared interest in using their rudimentary counselling training in responding informally, but more helpfully, to people in difficulties. As we discussed what they were doing and they deepened their understanding of counselling relationships, the issues of their roles and responsibilities had to be addressed. They were keen to extend the range and depth of their help, and gradually acquire facilities for doing so. We followed the pattern set in another nearby town where counselling had been embarked on eight years ago by the Council of Churches in similar *ad hoc* fashion. From that beginning there had developed a fully operational counselling service with premises and a team of experienced voluntary counsellors, with a grant from the local authority and paid staff. Initiatives like this are still occurring in other places.

STRENGTHS AND WEAKNESSES

It would be an oversimplification to try to discern too many clear patterns in the voluntary sector. There are so many variables which affect performance. Key individuals are one major influence. One or more enthusiastic, innovative members can give a dynamic lead and may inspire a thriving organization. Too much responsibility may devolve into too few hands. This leaves the organization very vulnerable, especially if one or two key people leave at the same time. The field staff of national organizations find that for every two local groups that are growing there is one which is in a period of decline, generally through loss of leadership or lack of resources. What are known as 'second-year blues' are a common phenomenon, when the enormous energy expended by a steering committee in setting up a new branch is followed by a sense of anti-climax and uncertainty about setting new objectives.

Standards of service are patchy. There is a high level of care and of understanding. All agencies are aware of the importance of giving time and attention to their clients, and train their counsellors to be good listeners. Counsellors offer time and a warm human response. But beyond that, aspirations vary. Not all seek to achieve the goal set out in the Isis centre, 'that the client should be able to understand his real feelings and bear to experience them, so that he may exercise conscious choices where he has hitherto been driven by motives of which he is not aware' (Oldfield 1983: 175). In other words, there is unanimity throughout the sector about providing counselling as a response to a crisis. But not all agencies are able to provide a service which can be classed as remedial or developmental, and not all open themselves to the scrutiny of external assessors.

Counselling agencies have to recognize that the offer to listen carries serious implications. Many counsellors listen very well, but are then uncertain how to respond to what they have heard. The counsellor feels the burden of the client's pain, and searches perhaps for a suitable referral for the client, believing that someone else will be a more effective source of help. The client fears that the problem he feels to be so overwhelming has also overwhelmed the counsellor. This can seem a barren point in counselling for both client and counsellor. Clients often give up counselling, leaving their counsellors with a sense of failure.

Counsellors need to gain the confidence to persevere even when their clients' despair or grief is great and they seem to be achieving nothing. They must come to terms with the fact that often there is nowhere else available to offer more effective help than their own. The best help may lie in just continuing to meet and being with the clients in their unresolved difficulties over a period. McLeod (1990b: 73) estimates that, for more than one-tenth of the time spent with clients, counsellors are faced with problems or dilemmas for which there are no obvious solutions, and the counsellors are uncertain about how to proceed. There is an obligation on any counselling agency to provide a caring environment in which the client's pain can be held, and to give support to the counsellor in this demanding commitment, so that the relationship between counsellor and client can bring relief and recuperation.

The intensity of client problems, and the consequent common feelings of inadequacy in counsellors, exert constant pressure on the voluntary sector to improve its standards. There is little sign of complacency. Most agencies continually try to upgrade the training and support for their workers, and strive to attract more input of professional expertise. Some medical, probation and social services allocate staff time for working with voluntary agencies. This is invaluable support. It would be a great asset if it were more widely available. When negotiating with statutory authorities for grants, counselling agencies can also press for assistance from skilled staff, for instance in running training sessions and supervision groups for volunteers. This is a very effective use of the time of social workers and psychologists. It enables their skill and insight to percolate widely through the voluntary workers. It makes a reality of partnership between the statutory and voluntary sectors. Many professionals contribute such help voluntarily, but official sanction and time allocated from their work schedule would enable their involvement to be planned with greater regularity and certainty.

Improvements are not without cost, however. Even when trainers are not paid, there are hidden financial costs in terms of travelling expenses, hire of rooms or equipment. There are also costs in terms of time and commitment. Though many counsellors are avid for new training opportunities, others are reluctant or unable to give up additional time, with the consequence that more time spent on training can mean less time for counselling. In agencies which have well-developed support systems, it is not uncommon for counsellors who undertake three counselling sessions a week to spend almost half as much time again in supervision or support groups.

These proportions raise the question of cost-effectiveness. Relate has faced these issues for some time. For many years its marriage counsellors and supervisors were unpaid. It then became apparent that a comprehensive supervisory system could only be achieved by paying supervisors. With such a level of support, it became desirable to ask counsellors to do more counselling and to pay them for doing sessions over and above their voluntary undertaking. The inevitable next step was to make full use of the experience of counsellors by creating salaried posts for those willing to undertake them. The pressure for improved standards created this progression, over the years, from a wholly voluntary service to a part-salaried one. This is a real dilemma. It raises the question of how we define what constitutes a volunteer.

Other external pressures are now appearing on the horizon for the voluntary sector. Individual counsellors are increasingly seeking recognition and status. National Vocational Qualifications are being developed which are based on demonstrated competence in specific skills. These are likely to differentiate between advice, guidance, befriending, counselling skills and counselling, with separate awards made (BAC 1992b: 130). BAC is revising its accreditation standards, but the requirements remain too demanding for virtually all voluntary counsellors. All these awards will be valued by the recipients, but the time and cost of implementing the necessary procedures will be enormous, and the voluntary sector is unlikely to concern itself with them. There is also a growing interest in integration of counselling and psychotherapy standards within Europe, which raises issues for the counselling profession. Those developments may seem of little relevance at present to the voluntary sector, but may well have implications, not yet foreseen, by the turn of the century.

Throughout the United Kingdom there is a massive increase in the number of educational institutions offering counselling courses, many of them awarding their own certificates or diplomas. Some are subsidized through adult education departments; some, such as Metanoia and the Westminster Pastoral Foundation, charge substantial fees; some, such as Open University modules, form part of more extensive education courses. These courses increase the pool of potential counsellors with some training available to voluntary counselling agencies. Some agencies have recruited successfully from these sources. Several are able to offer student placements to the trainees for their practical experience during their course. That arrangement can prove a great asset both to the agency and to the students.

However, these opportunities pose problems for the established specialist organizations. Agencies can only take students if they have an office base, staffed while the students are working, and if they can provide sufficient and frequent supervision for them. As for recruiting counsellors from external courses, the agencies need to have sufficiently sophisticated selection procedures to assess the competence of such recruits and decide whether or not they need to undergo the full training laid on in the agency for other new counsellors. The orientation and expectations of these already certificated counsellors may differ markedly from those of the untrained volunteers that have traditionally been enlisted, and the new calibre of volunteer can serve as an uncomfortable lever of change upon the existing system.

These developments at national and international level again highlight the paradox in the voluntary counselling sector that the help given is instinctively amateur yet also quasi-professional. Writing over 30 years ago about community mental health, Caplan (1961: 21) warned of the risk of many different professions emerging, each with their own standardized range of ways of handling their professional problems. He argued for the importance of preserving flexibility and 'individual variation according to the idiosyncratic personality structure of the individual professional worker'.

Caplan also warns against training that can undermine the spontaneity of workers and rob them of their confidence. He speculated that social workers were escaping from the field into their offices because things were becoming too complicated:

> Once upon a time, if you went on a home visit and someone offered you a cup of coffee and you wanted to be nice and polite, you took it. Nowadays you have to think, 'Well, what does this mean? She offers me a cup of coffee on this visit but she didn't do this last time. What does it mean that she leaves the door of the room open? . . . What does it mean that "by chance" she has neighbours visiting her? What does it mean that there's someone there in the corner she doesn't

introduce me to?' These used not to be problems. Now they are very complicated problems.

(Caplan 1961: 192)

Counselling easily falls into this trap of making things too complicated. The voluntary sector has to be particularly conscious of guarding against it in its continuing endeavour to borrow what is best from professional practice and adapt it for use by 'amateurs'. Voluntary agencies should be able to retain the flexibility of 'amateurishness'. They are free of statutory constraints so can take more risks, and respond more readily to new needs. They sometimes go where statutory agencies fear to tread. Government departments are often glad to give pump-priming grants so that new schemes can first be tested out in the voluntary sector. Though some agencies may be very set in their ways, the sector itself is able to be innovative and to respond flexibly by taking initiatives to tackle new issues of social concern.

CO-OPERATION IN THE NETWORK

The picture presented by the voluntary counselling network is of a multitude of autonomous organizations, often fiercely independent, often ill informed about other counselling services. Those in the large national organizations, with a network of local branches, may feel more strongly allied to their specialist network than to other counselling agencies in their own vicinity. Institutional anxieties, loyalty to the parent body, local rivalries and a desire for independence prove stronger instincts than a wish to share resources.

At a national level, amalgamations among organizations fulfilling related tasks are rare. They are only likely to be brought about by external pressure, such as from funding bodies as a condition of continued grants. While I was working at the NMGC, we were disappointed that, for reasons on both sides, collaborative relationships on some aspects of our activities were not achieved with the Catholic Marriage Advisory Council. Both of the organizations had a network throughout the United Kingdom of counselling centres and local training, and both had a spread of centrally trained tutors undertaking the supervision of counsellors also nation-wide. We shared the common focus of marital work and a common philosophy of client-centred counselling. A small degree of collaboration was achieved through occasional joint training for tutors, and, in one or two places, by secondment of counsellors between agencies. But

these remained as pioneer projects which were left as local initiatives, or later lapsed. They could have been built on. There was
potential for further joint use of trained personnel and premises,
and there was a staff structure that could have achieved it. Yet we
never managed to give high enough priority to the hard work and
commitment which were required to use those experimental projects
as stepping-stones towards closer collaboration between the two
national organizations.

Some successful attempts have been made to bring agencies closer
together at a local level. For example, in Exeter, a pleasant old
block of almshouses has been transformed by the local authority
into offices for a dozen local voluntary organizations, enabling many
of the helping agencies to be situated in proximity around a small
courtyard. Similarly, in Newcastle upon Tyne, Mea House was
purpose built in the city centre to house about twenty voluntary
agencies. And, more recently, in Milton Keynes the new city-centre
church has been built to incorporate joint premises for voluntary
bodies. Each agency maintains its separate existence, but they share
common facilities such as meeting rooms and expensive office
equipment.

Such geographical proximity has advantages. It makes the organizations more aware and knowledgeable about each other. It
encourages informal communication between staff members of the
various agencies. Clients may also become more conscious of the
range of services available for them. Agencies which are dealing
with the same families can exchange information conveniently,
within the limits of confidentiality. Referral of clients between
agencies can be achieved through personal introductions.

However, the advantages do not stretch much beyond improve-
ment of informal relationships. There seems little attempt to collaborate at a significant technical level. Volunteers continue to be
selected and trained unilaterally. Agencies still offer their services
independently, and working partnerships between agencies have
not been fostered.

Joint ventures in the voluntary sector are rare. In one or two
places efforts have been successfully made which show that it is
possible to cross inter-agency boundaries, and have confirmed that
it is desirable to do so. Scotland has taken a lead in this. In rural
areas there, all agencies face problems in providing a service for
small numbers of people in isolated communities. The Confederation of Scottish Counselling Agencies (COSCA) serves as a forum
for encouraging the main counselling bodies to plan a joint service
in some districts. The pioneer venture is in Skye, where the Marriage

Counselling Service, the Council for Alcoholism and Cruse planned a project for recruiting and training counsellors generically to serve the three agencies. In the event Cruse had to withdraw because the churches considered their own help with bereavement was sufficient, but the other two agencies continued together. The three organizations are working on a similar venture in Stornoway and Benbecula in the Outer Hebrides. Such communities are too small to support three agencies, but, working together, a generic service maintaining the essential specialisms can be established.

Entirely different factors pertained in Dover to produce a similar outcome. Dover was the home port of the *Herald of Free Enterprise*, and the sinking of that ferry had a major impact on the town. An emergency service was set up to assist victims. Over the following two years extensive efforts were made by the staff of the service to follow up all those involved in the disaster, and most of them were interviewed and counselled. Some of this counselling was long-term and needed to be continued even after the emergency service had fulfilled its main purpose and was disbanded. Continuing provision had to be made for these long-term clients.

The new agency that grew out of the emergency service became the Dover Counselling Centre. It began in 1989, opening its doors to new clients as well as continuing ones. It provides both generic and specialist help. The Centre acts as the local branch of Cruse, Relate and the Council on Addiction. The separate identity of each of these participating agencies is preserved, each with its own structure and its own counsellors. However, the three groups of counsellors work together as a team. They all share additional training, and have supervision in common. The experienced counsellors are all on the rota to provide general counselling for any clients who require counselling other than in one of the specialisms.

The Dover Centre is thus providing a full range of counselling. Important categories of clients who do not fit into the normal parameters of the specialist services are those with problems of redundancy, abuse involving both sexes, debt, unemployment and sexual problems of individuals. A support line is also available for employees of Kent County Council, which is made possible financially by a grant from the Council. Additional training and supervision enable the experienced counsellors of the separate agencies to help such clients across the whole spectrum of problems without having to refer elsewhere.

This pattern could well be emulated in towns elsewhere. It combines the advantage of providing a generic service while preserving the advantage of proven specialist help. This achievement has come about through sincere and intensive attempts at grappling with the inter-agency anxieties and dynamics (Woodhouse and Pengelly 1991) mentioned in Chapter 5. All the parties acknowledge the different standards and competences in the three agencies, and work together to accommodate each other, and where necessary learn the value of compromise.

This multi-agency centre became possible because an opportunity was presented and the right personnel were in place at that time. The first organizer, Janet Johnston, was an experienced social worker with extensive experience of work in voluntary agencies. She was able to bring her knowledge of both sectors to bear in building bridges across them. Such collaboration is difficult to achieve without external pressures of some sort, though it would be pessimistic to conclude that it can only be achieved in the wake of a major disaster!

The lesson from Dover is that partnership within the voluntary sector can be achieved. The success of the Dover Counselling Centre should inspire voluntary organizations elsewhere to explore the benefits that can flow from such increased collaboration.

EVALUATION

A notable weakness in the voluntary sector is the lack of attention paid to research and evaluation of counselling. Counsellors spend much time and attention on their clients. They meet regularly in case discussion groups to examine their work with clients, to assist them in understanding themselves and their clients better, and to consider different ways of providing therapeutic help. This reflection and examination of individual clients is a basic element in the counselling process. Yet systematic attempts to evaluate the outcome of counselling for a sizeable population are few and far between.

There are several reasons for this lack of research. Agencies such as the alcohol and drug organizations deal with clients who move around frequently and are difficult to trace. Others, such as the marriage and family ones, normally deal with one or two members of a family only and fear confidentiality may be breached through follow-up. Many are so pressed by the immediate issues that evaluation studies seem too costly in terms of time and effort, or are a diversion from work with people in current difficulties.

For those agencies which set out to undertake evaluation, methodological problems abound. Is it feasible to plan a survey

which satisfies scientific scrutiny, in which a sample group who
have been counselled can be matched with a control group who
have not? How can a group of clients be identified who are representative of the total client population? Should interviews with ex-
clients be structured or open-ended? What objective measurement
of outcome can be devised?

Most of the existing studies dwell at length on methodological
hazards. Such accounts are of value in themselves, for they often
throw new light on the complexity of the helping process, but de-
finite results are hard to determine. Writers on research conclude
that the degree of rigour required in the physical sciences is impossible to achieve in social science research (Bolger 1991: 390;
Home Office and DHSS 1979: Chapter 8).

Counsellors have additional hurdles to overcome. They may fear
that attempts at evaluating counselling by a third party will inter-
fere with the effects of their therapy or revive painful issues for
their clients. They may consider that the mental health or family
circumstances of particular clients make it inappropriate for them
to be approached by a research worker. They may feel that the
outcome of their 'therapeutic alliance' is too unspecific to be measured, or that their clients' views about what was or was not achieved
are likely to be too subjective to be of value.

Nevertheless, follow-up studies of some client groups in Britain
have been undertaken. The most comprehensive are those by Mayer
and Timms (1970), who interviewed 61 clients of the Family Welfare
Association; by Oldfield (1983), with 52 clients at the Isis counselling centre in Oxford; and by Hunt (1985), who interviewed 51 out
of a cohort of 141 clients who attended the Manchester MGC in
October and November 1980.

The conclusions of these studies are mixed and tentative. Half of
Hunt's sample were very satisfied with their counselling, and a further quarter felt that some benefits had accrued from it. Their assessments of the outcome were linked to their initial expectations,
particularly in relation to whether or not their marriages could be
'saved'. In addition to evaluating outcome, the ex-clients expressed
many varied views about counselling. Sometimes critical comments
were directed at the setting in which the counselling took place,
rather than at the counsellor. Often it was difficult to disentangle
the influence of the counselling from the effect of other significant
events happening in the clients' lives at the same time. Nevertheless,
a picture has been built up of how clients experience counselling.
As McLeod (1990a: 19) puts it: 'This is research which gives the
client a voice. No longer would the clients' view be filtered through

the screen of scientific method. And who really knows where that might lead?'

Not all evaluation needs to be undertaken on a large scale. Small agencies can embark on their own follow-up. Postal questionnaires sent to clients some months after completion of counselling may elicit useful feedback, though the response may be disappointingly low. Incidentally, such follow-up enquiries are often interpreted by clients as a welcome sign of continuing concern for them.

One such simple questionnaire was sent by a new branch of Cruse in Weston-super-Mare to its first 40 clients. The questionnaire comprised four closed questions on a four-point scale (such as 'If a friend were in need of similar help would you recommend Cruse to him/her?'), and three open questions for fuller comments (such as 'What aspects of counselling by Cruse were helpful? . . . and unhelpful?').

Twenty questionnaires were returned completed (a 50% response rate is good). Only four of the respondents were not satisfied with the counselling they received. Most of the remainder were very satisfied. The open questions produced suggestions about practical arrangements, personal reactions to the service offered, and comments about the counsellors. This modest exercise raised questions about the 50% who did not reply, but the input from users was helpful in planning the development of the service.

Alternative strategies for evaluation have been proposed. Sutton (1987) advocates a quite different, more immediate method. She encourages counsellors to evaluate the effectiveness of their own counselling as they proceed, by making regular assessments jointly with their clients at intervals throughout the counselling. Together counsellor and client can set counselling goals, and at intervals they can assess the extent to which these goals are being achieved. Progress may turn out to be straightforward or erratic, and the goals can be extended or modified. By making the goals specific it is possible to measure how far they have been attained. This approach not only enables a service to be evaluated, but also has additional benefits of involving counsellors in the evaluation of their own activities, as well as assisting them in clarifying the focus of their counselling.

Research is important in other areas, too. Training courses and supervision can be evaluated, both through issuing satisfaction questionnaires to participants after the event, and, more usefully, through attempts to measure what skills have been acquired. One study set out to discover gaps in bereavement training. Postal questionnaires were sent to practising counsellors asking them to identify an incident of particular difficulty they had experienced in counselling (Stock 1991). Over one hundred counsellors replied. Though this was a random sample of counsellors, it proved possible to verify that the clients on which the counsellors based their replies were representative of the overall clientele of the agency. From this small study it became clear that extra support was required for counsellors when dealing with certain categories of client – in effect, those with a psychiatric history; those who became over-dependent; suicidal and angry clients; and clients who were classified as 'stuck'.

Research may seem a grandiose aim or even a threatening subject to voluntary counselling bodies. It is likely to be resented by practitioners, especially if other people set out to evaluate their work without adequate explanation. Administrators may co-operate half-heartedly, especially if a burden of additional work falls on them when they are not fully consulted about its purpose. But as long as the extra work entailed does not seem out of proportion to any results likely to emerge from it, co-operation can be gained from people who are convinced of the point of the research.

The studies mentioned here show that small-scale projects are possible and worthwhile. They can be carried out by practitioners already working in the agency, or can be a fruitful field of collaboration with research workers from outside institutions. The expense need not be great. The results often throw useful light on aspects of service delivery. More particularly, the exercise can prove a stimulating one in itself. The work involved in thinking and planning, in drawing up the project, agreeing the methodology, and involving counsellors and clients in its progress can all contribute to creating a positive atmosphere of critical enquiry throughout the whole of an organization.

EQUAL OPPORTUNITIES

The requirements of equal opportunities legislation offer major challenges to counselling agencies, in all three areas of gender and sexual orientation, disability and racial awareness. All counselling agencies accept the principles behind the various anti-discriminatory Acts, and many have issued statements of intent to work towards the full requirements. These requirements are, however, complex and often costly to put into practice – such as premises where access and all facilities are available for staff and clients in wheelchairs; and recruitment practice which conforms to the guidelines on equal opportunity interviews to ensure there is no overt or covert discrimination against any candidate.

As well as overcoming these outward and visible signs of discrimination, organizations have to understand their own innate prejudices. Coate (1991: 15) describes the process she experienced as the Westminster Pastoral Foundation grappled with these 'less tangible and sometimes extremely painful issues':

> We have discovered a need for education of ourselves at a much deeper level; and that it is easy to accept an equal opportunities principle, but takes much individual and corporate soul-searching to achieve good working practices ...
> The overall challenge is both extensive and intensive.

Her colleague, Duckworth (1991: 6), writes of her first experience of interviewing two deaf applicants for a course – one required an interpreter throughout and the other could lipread, could partially hear with a loop, and could speak. Her difficulty lay in having to come to terms with her own feelings and ignorance about deafness. An unsighted marriage counsellor spoke of the distrust he experienced in an organization which laid great store on the importance of visual contact and in which he felt himself a guinea-pig. He had a problem in persuading selectors that what he lacked in sight was compensated for by heightened sensitivity elsewhere. He had long service as a very effective counsellor. His only difficulty lay in the initial uncertainty of clients who were not used to blind people, and their surprise at seeing a dog in the room (Nussbaum 1976).

These practitioners emphasize the importance of familiarizing oneself with the unfamiliar, in order to free oneself from fear of the unknown. Such fears also need to be faced in other areas. People working with clients with learning difficulties need to be comfortable about body contact; those dealing with relationships must be at ease with transvestism or homosexuality, and able to be explicit about physical and emotional aspects of sex; those working in the field of terminal illness need to be familiar with pain and with dead and mutilated bodies.

What is important for counsellors is equally important for their organizations. The danger is that they may not know of their own ignorance. Much discrimination is covert, unrecognized by the agency itself. It is all too easy to advertise for counsellors only in areas where recruitment has been successful before, and thus inadvertently perpetuate a counselling team with similar backgrounds. It is all too common to have inaccessible premises, necessitating different arrangements for the partially mobile which may cause them embarrassment and act as a deterrent to their persevering with counselling.

An agency's discriminatory bias is likely to be reflected in the composition of its management committee. I recollect serving on one committee which always had to await the arrival of the Dial-a-Ride bus and which met on the ground floor. We were much preoccupied with finding new premises, and had several tempting offers to move to offices which were ideal in every respect except ease of access. Temptation was only resisted because we had a constant reminder in our midst that such premises would not be satisfactory. On another occasion, one member of a management committee, drawing on personal experience, held up the appointment of a new organizer until such time as the full equal opportunities procedure had been followed. That involved much extra time and effort; and no little exasperation. It resulted, however, in the appointment of someone with a different ethnic background who then radically challenged many of the assumptions in the agency. Neither of these outcomes would have been achieved with a committee with monochrome composition.

Achieving a committee membership which has informed input on many of these issues is not easy. Committees can be motivated by the letter of the equal opportunities legislation rather than its spirit, and look for token representatives of minority groups. It is never easy to be a lone representative on a committee, and doubly difficult if one feels one is there merely as a token gesture to gender, race or social group.

First and foremost, what is required by management committees is a profound conviction of the need for other perspectives. People should be asked to serve because it is recognized that they have an important contribution to make, not just as a token minority representative. Secretaries of ethnic organizations tend to be wary of the offers they receive to nominate a member to serve on committees. They get many such requests, often from organizations which have not gone to any trouble to make personal contact in advance. Such offers are seen as attempts to get a token black face on a committee and, quite reasonably, may be ignored. A positive response is only likely to result when time and trouble is taken by the inviting body to find out who is the most appropriate person to approach, then to meet to discuss the request and explore together why and what sort of help is needed.

It is vital in our increasingly pluralist society that efforts are made by counselling organizations to grapple with the barriers that prevent the development of truly multi-cultural counselling services. In the same way that a choice should be available as to whether to go to a specialist or a generic agency, so there should be choice of agencies for clients from ethnic minorities. There is a continuing and important role for the Asian Family Counselling Service, where clients and counsellors choose to work within their own cultural setting. But clients and counsellors of all cultures who prefer to work in other generic agencies should be free to do so. Great strides still need to be made in multi-cultural understanding, and it is to be hoped that ill-informed or unwelcoming responses from the generic agencies will become rarer, and that clients and prospective counsellors will not feel excluded from them.

Experience in the Association of Black Counsellors and elsewhere has shown that counselling and therapeutic help are effective across racial divides. For over a decade the Nafsiyat centre, which owed its inspiration to the late Jafar Kareem, has been committed to developing a range of therapeutic approaches for members of black and minority ethnic groups. The centre lays emphasis on a sharing of power between therapist and client, conscious of the need not only to work on the client's inner traumas, but also on what Kareem called 'the external monsters' of poverty, violence and injustice. Nafsiyat combines keen political awareness and therapeutic innovation, and recruits its staff accordingly. It welcomes white therapists from a diversity of cultural and language backgrounds who are prepared to work inter-culturally. While its clientele remains socially disadvantaged, it will continue to provide its specialist and unique service. Its long-term aim is to fulfil the hope of its founder that such 'a separate service would be temporary and, ultimately, unnecessary' (*Guardian* 1992).

Though ignorance and discrimination may be visible in relation to ethnic minorities, organizations also have class distinctions which are equally strong but less apparent. The voluntary sector has had a struggle to free itself from its middle-class, do-gooding image. To a large extent that process has been one of change in the nature of the do-gooding, rather than of the class of people who actually do it. The paternalistic notion of helpers as superior beings who know what is best for unfortunate victims, has given way to a relationship of greater equality based on principles of client autonomy and self-regulation. But many agencies still largely rely on volunteers from the educated middle class, where the tradition of voluntary service persists.

Many excellent counsellors are recruited from this traditional source. The danger is that the strength of this tradition itself can act in a discriminatory fashion against potential volunteers from other backgrounds. The more that is required of volunteers in terms of, for instance, residential training, the more difficult it becomes for people who have not had the benefit of tertiary education to take the risk of offering themselves. In this regard voluntary agencies face the same problems as the Open University, which sets out to recruit people who have not had previous further educational opportunities, but in fact attracts students largely from teaching, nursing and other professions.

Some of the newer counselling agencies have been successful in recruiting across the socio-economic divides. This most frequently happens in counselling services which grow out of self-help groups, since the experiences which bring members to such groups, such as grief, domestic violence or sexual assaults, occur across all social divides. Other agencies successfully draw from sources that have no tradition of voluntary social service, such as Restart courses and the Pre-School Playgroup movement, which has a remarkable record in discovering and developing young parents with previously un-recognized managerial or caring skills. Some communities have un-tapped abilities waiting to be uncovered, as was shown during the miners' strike of 1984 when the miners' wives found themselves driven to take action against pit closures. As a result of the increased self-confidence which they discovered through their picketing and lobbying, a whole range of new opportunities opened up for them, many in the voluntary sector. Government should take care that its fiscal and social policies do not have the effect of preventing new groups in the community from taking a full part in voluntary organizations.

The voluntary sector sometimes fights shy of facing these class differences, but it has to be acknowledged that they exist. The issue is particularly acute where professional standards are expected from volunteers who receive no payment. To be able to give time and skill voluntarily is a luxury which is denied to a lot of people with low incomes and little social support. Voluntary counselling organ-izations have to live with this unwelcome reality. The utopia is far distant when the quasi-professional counselling undertaken by vol-unteers will be acknowledged to be of sufficient worth to be paid for as part of the official state caring network. As in all other areas of discrimination, agencies have a duty to educate themselves about these issues, and pursue policies that aim to create opportunities that are as equal as possible for clients, volunteers, staff and committee members.

SUMMARY

At whatever level it pitches its service, any agency which sets out to provide personal help based on counselling skills and understanding, needs to satisfy itself that it is attending to key managerial and technical functions. A checklist for such self-appraisal could consist of 12 headings: five relating to management, which I have adapted from Poulton (1988: 162), and seven to technical performance. Those relating to management functions are as follows:

1 Resources – an agency must find and maintain its funding, premises and other essential resources in order to run its entire organization.
2 Staffing – an agency must appoint a viable management committee, and needs to recruit and support staff.
3 Legal – an agency must carry out its legal responsibilities as an employer and in relation to the Companies Act and the Charity Commissioners.
4 Promotional – an agency needs to provide accurate information to the public, relevant professions and other agencies.
5 Policy – an agency must formulate its policy in conjunction with all sections of its membership.

Those relating to technical functions are as follows:

6 Selection – an agency needs a systematic selection process which safeguards the agency, the clients and the candidates.
7 Basic training – an agency must ensure that all counsellors undergo a recognized training and satisfy trainers of their competence.
8 Supervision – an agency should provide regular supervision for all counsellors regardless of their length of experience.
9 In-service training – an agency needs to create opportunities for updating and refreshing all counsellors.
10 Clients – an agency must provide confidential counselling, flexible enough to meet the needs of clients appropriate to the agency.
11 Referral – an agency must make provision for referral of clients, and for ending counselling of those for whom it is no longer appropriate or who might be better served elsewhere.
12 Records – an agency should maintain a system of client records as considered necessary, and ensure their confidentiality.

CONCLUSION

Voluntary organizations that use counselling as a principal means of helping individuals and groups are flourishing. They continue to grow in number and to attract an increasing body of counsellors and new clients. Their scope is wide and their response to problems of emotional and mental health is diverse. Much of this growth has been initiated and nurtured by the established helping professions. It is the realization of a scenario envisaged over thirty years ago by Caplan (1961: 201–2).

> We must work out methods whereby a small number of highly trained people can work with the many caretaking agents of a community who are in so strategic a position during crisis periods to affect the mental health of so large a proportion of the community. If we can succeed in working out some techniques of this nature and if we can get ourselves trained in it, we shall have developed for the very first time a potent instrument whereby we may achieve some kind of approximation of community coverage.

Counselling does not claim to have a monopoly in achieving this goal, since other forms of voluntary community involvement are also essential. But it is a major 'technique'. It has evolved relevant training. And it has a strategic 'instrument' through its service network for dealing with personal crisis and, furthermore, with issues of personal growth. Its practice is not confined to counselling rooms, nor to telephone helplines, nor to prearranged home visits. It percolates through as a supportive way of responding personally to people in emotional pain by those who have had counselling training, by retired counsellors and by those who have learnt to listen and understand better by having been clients themselves. Much effective help is given through 'counselling on the hoof' in schools and colleges, hospital wards, beauty salons, funeral parlours or over the garden fence.

In a paper on differentiating between counselling and psychotherapy, Thorne (1992) concluded that attempts to make a rigid divide were both 'fruitless and dangerous'. He pleaded with counsellors not to undervalue themselves in comparison with psychotherapists. In this book I have been more conscious of the possible divide at the other end of the counselling continuum, between those officially called 'counsellors' and those with labels such as 'visitor' or 'befriender'. My plea to them is not to undervalue themselves in comparison with qualified counsellors. What matters

is that we all take the opportunities offered to us, in whatever
setting, to do the best that we can, and that we struggle together
'to lay hold on internal reality, to transform suffering and to heal
wounds, to foster authenticity and to risk intimacy, to discover
spirit and to find meaning' (Thorne 1992: 247).

I have argued that the growth of a wide range of counselling
services is commendable, a sign of a compassionate society whose
traditional supports are increasingly failing and which seeks for new
ones. Three caveats must be entered. The first is that counselling
has its limitations. Its disciples, in their enthusiasm, may close their
eyes to them. But agencies must be alert to the fact that not all pain
is psychological, and that the talking cure is of secondary value
where distress stems from physical causes. Counsellors require a
proper humility as well as a proper confidence, and should seek
second opinions if in any doubt.

Second, the political dimension must be borne in mind. One
aspect of this is that the voluntary sector is leaned on too heavily,
and the goodwill of its volunteers is exploited. This is only possible
because of the traditional discrimination against women who form
the major section of the counselling workforce. Society, in the form
of its mouthpiece, the government, will get away with paying as
little as possible for its counselling service for as long as it can. In
the political climate of the 1990s, the existence of the voluntary
organizations is a convenient alibi for cutting back the statutory
personal social services.

Third, and again politically, counselling in some contexts may be
a distraction in a world which needs to struggle for justice, peace
and equality. Counselling agencies can be seen as the emotional
equivalent of international aid agencies. The latter bring sacks of
grain to starving populations while discriminatory tariffs operate
against the governments of those countries. In similar fashion,
counsellors may merely be bringing emotional comfort to clients
whose problems are more deeply rooted in social and economic
deprivation. People who are deprived of the basic conditions of time
and space, money and education may lack the power within
themselves to change their lifestyles. Priority for them may entail
change in their environment (Smail 1984).

Counsellors tend not to be political beings. But the neutrality of
the counselling room should not inhibit counsellors from actively
espousing political causes with which they come face to face through
counselling. I find it encouraging that the British Association of
Counselling has working groups on such political issues as justice,
race and disability. Counsellors have taken social action in various

spheres. Those working with service personnel or uniformed services after military or civil disasters have been moved to campaign for official recognition of the effects of post-traumatic stress disorder. Marriage and family counsellors, facing the at times irreconcilable pulls of encouraging individual autonomy and helping people to adjust within traditional family structures, have actively campaigned for the liberalization of divorce laws and increasing social security benefits. Housing injustices which have increasingly been revealed in Citizens' Advice Bureaux have caused CAB workers to change their help from merely giving advice to taking on adversarial roles on behalf of their clients. Tensions are experienced acutely by counsellors working in the Muslim community where the issue of how far to adapt to British customs and laws is extremely contentious.

The counselling world is not immune from political issues. Indeed, counsellors should work to have more of a political voice. The argument that establishing a counselling service is a ploy for dealing with their mistakes by incompetent managers or impotent politicians is overstating the case. Nevertheless, the point is valid that a newly discovered need may be inappropriately met merely by providing counselling, rather than openly fighting the social conditions which have given rise to the need. The 'external monsters' of Jafar Kareem, to whom I referred above, are still very alive. We should follow his lead in openly fighting injustice at the same time as providing counselling for its casualties.

These are important caveats. They are not sufficient to invalidate the strength and usefulness of the voluntary counselling sector. Its vitality and its value lie in the diversity of its provision. Though this diversity throughout the sector means that standards vary and do not command universal acceptance in all of the agencies, the network as a whole offers a variety which matches the variety of clients seeking help. We should be less concerned about working towards greater uniformity in agencies than about seeking more effective ways of enabling potential clients to find the help that is right for them. With this aim we can all rejoice at the variety that is available.

I cannot put a financial estimate on the value of this help. Attempts have been made from time to time to prove that counselling is cost-effective. That may be true. Such estimates are generally special pleading, however, used by agencies who need to back their application for public funds with claims of savings on psychotrophic drugs, medical consultations, sickness benefit and hospitalization. Such claims can only be speculative. In fact, counselling is highly labour-intensive and, if all counsellors were salaried, it would be impossible for the health service to fund more than a small proportion of the current volume of counselling.

The arguments about cost-effectiveness remain inconclusive. One research study concluded that the case was not proven that the voluntary sector is more cost-effective or innovative than the statutory sector (Brenton 1985: 194). However, the author went on to commend the achievements of voluntary agencies working in areas of mutual aid, self-help, community and neighbourhood action and advice services (Brenton 1985: 220). These are precisely the areas in which counselling flourishes.

Counselling is both a healing and a preventive process. It aims to help people to function more effectively, to promote mental health and prevent unhealthy dependence. It plays a significant part in countering stress-related disease and in fostering social and spiritual welfare. This probably results in great savings to the public purse, but the benefits cannot be measured.

The real justification for counselling lies not in financial terms. It rests in the massively growing demand for the services of counsellors; in the benefits experienced by many of the recipients of counselling; and in the gains from training felt by counsellors and the many other students who become involved in counselling courses.

Faced with human distress, present-day counsellors feel the same imperative as their forebears to 'needs try'. The pioneers acted out of ignorance, but they had abundant goodwill. Today's counsellors have the advantage of being able to make a considered response based on the experience and the cumulative wisdom of counselling that has been gained in many settings for over half a century. Much of this experience and wisdom emanates from the voluntary sector.

All the signs point to a great increase in these needs during the next half-century. The clocks will not be put back to a time when families and neighbours take responsibility for their suffering members. Neither the state nor the private sector is able to shoulder this massive burden of care. The voluntary sector will be needed, in ever greater numbers, to provide a mosaic of varied and increasingly sophisticated counselling services. To staff them, it will continue to rely on volunteers to undertake counselling in many different settings, and to maintain the services for the community of which they can be justly proud.

Appendix: addresses of voluntary counselling organizations

Albany Trust
  24 Chester Sq, London SW1W 9HS
  (071) 730 5871
Alcohol Concern
  305 Gray's Inn Rd, London WC1X 8QF
  (071) 833 3471
Asian Family Counselling Service
  74 The Avenue, Ealing, London W13 8LB
  (081) 997 5749, and
  Equity Chambers, 40 Piccadilly, Bradford BD1 3NN
  (0274) 720486
BACUP (British Association of Cancer United Patients)
  121–123 Charterhouse St, London EC1M 6AA
  (071) 608 1038
British Association for Counselling
  1 Regent Place, Rugby, Warwicks CV21 2PJ
  (0788) 578328
Catholic Marriage Advisory Council
  Clitherow House, 1 Blythe Mews, Blythe Rd, London W14 0NW
  (071) 371 1341
Cerebral Palsy Helpline
  c/o Spastics Society, 12 Park Crescent, London W1N 4EQ
  (0800) 626216
Compassionate Friends
  6 Denmark St, Bristol BS1 5DQ
  (0272) 292778
Confederation of Scottish Counselling Agencies
  64 Murray Place, Stirling FK8 2BX
  (0786) 75140

Cruse Bereavement Care
  126 Sheen Rd, Richmond, Surrey TW9 1UR
  (081) 940 4818
Dover Counselling Centre
  9 Cambridge Terrace, Dover, Kent CT16 1YZ
  (0304) 204123
Duchesne Muscular Dystrophy Support Group
  c/o Nattrass House, 35 Macaulay House, London SW4 0QP
  (071) 226 2673
Families Need Fathers
  BM Families, London WC1N 3XX
  (081) 886 0970
Family Welfare Association
  501–505 Kingsland Rd, London E8 4AU
  (071) 402 6251
Grail, The
  Waxwell Farm House, 125 Waxwell Lane, Pinner, Mddx HA5 3ER
  (081) 866 0505
Hospice Information Service
  St Christopher's Hospice, 51–59 Lawrie Park Rd, London SE26 6DZ
  (081) 778 9252
Isis Centre
  Dartington House, Little Clarendon St, Oxford
  0865 56648
Jewish Marriage Council
  23 Ravenshurst Avenue, London NW4 4EE
  (081) 203 6311
Miscarriage Association
  PO Box 40 Ossett, West Yorks WF5 9XG
  (0924) 830515
Myalgic Encephalomyelitis Association
  Stanhope House, High St, Stanford-le-Hope, Essex SS17 0HA
  (0375) 642466
Nafsiyat
  278 Seven Sisters Rd, London N4 2HY
  (071) 263 4130
National Association of Bereavement Services
  20 Norton Folgate, Bishopgate, London E1 6DB
  (071) 247 0617
National Association of Citizens Advice Bureaux
  115–123 Pentonville Rd, London N1 9LZ
  (071) 833 2181
National Association of Widows
  54–57 Allison St, Digbeth, Birmingham B5 5TH
  (021) 643 8348
National Council of Voluntary Child Care Organisations
  8 Wakley St, London EC1V 7QE
  (071) 833 3319

National Council of Voluntary Organisations
  26 Bedford Sq, London WC1B 3HU
  (071) 636 4066
National Family Conciliation Council
  Shaftesbury Centre, Percy St, Swindon SN2 2AZ
  (0793) 514055
Open Door
  De Broome Building, Boundaries Rd, Feltham, Middlesex TW13 5DT
  (081) 844 0309
Pregnancy Advisory Service
  13 Charlotte St, London W1P 1HD
  (071) 637 8962
Relate (National Marriage Guidance Council)
  Herbert Gray College, Little Church St, Rugby CV21 3AP
  (0788) 573241
Release
  388 Old St, London EC1V 9LT
  (071) 729 9904
SAFTA (Support Following Termination After Foetal Abnormality)
  29–30 Soho Sq, London W1V 6JB
  (071) 439 6124
Salvation Army Counselling Service
  105 Judd St, London WC1H 9TS
  (071) 247 0669
Samaritans
  17 Uxbridge Rd, Slough SL1 1SN
  (0753) 32713
Saneline
  c/o SANE, 2nd floor, 199 Old Marylebone Rd, London NW1 5QP
  (071) 724 8000
SPOD (Sexual and Personal Relationships of People with a Disability)
  286 Camden Rd, London N7 0BJ
  (071) 607 8851
Stepfamily (National Stepfamily Association)
  72 Willesden Lane, London NW6 7TA
  (071) 372 0846
Stillbirth and Neo-natal Death Society
  28 Portland Place, London W1N 4DE
  (071) 436 5881
Swindon Counselling Service
  23 Bath Rd, Swindon SN1 4AS
  (0793) 514550
Tavistock Institute of Marital Studies
  120 Belsize Lane, London NW3 5BA
  (071) 435 7111
Terrence Higgins Trust
  52–54 Gray's Inn Rd, London WC1X 8JU
  (071) 242 1010

Turning Point
  New Loom House, 101 Back Church Lane, London E1 1LU
  (071) 702 2300
Victim Support
  Cranmer House, 39 Brixton Rd, London SW9 6DZ
  (071) 735 9166
Wantage Counselling Service
  9 Church St, Wantage, Oxon OX12 8DL
  (02357) 69744
Westminster Pastoral Foundation
  23 Kensington Sq, London W8 5HN
  (071) 937 6956
Youth Access–Counselling and Advisory Services (formerly NAYPCAS)
  11 Newarke St, Leicester LE1 5SS
  (0533) 558763

References

Alcohol Concern (1989) *Training Volunteer Alcohol Counsellors: The Minimum Standards*. London: Alcohol Concern.

Alcohol Concern (1991) *Training Guidelines*. London: Alcohol Concern.

Alcohol Concern (1992) *Involving Volunteer Counsellors*. London: Alcohol Concern.

Allen, L. (1990) 'A client's experience of failure', in Mearns, D. and Dryden, W. (eds), *Experiences of Counselling in Action*. London: Sage.

Balint, M. (1964) *The Doctor, His Patient and the Illness*. Tunbridge Wells: Pitman Medical.

Belbin, R. (1981) *Management Teams*. London: Heinemann.

Berne, E. (1964) *Games People Play*. Harmondsworth: Penguin.

Black, D. (1991) *A Place for Exploration*. London: Westminster Pastoral Foundation/SPCK.

Bolger, T. (1991) 'Research and evaluation in counselling', in Dryden, W. et al. (eds), *Handbook of Counselling in Britain*. London: Routledge.

Bowlby, J. (1969) *Attachment and Loss*. London: Hogarth Press.

Bowlby, J. (1979) *The Making and Breaking of Affectional Bonds*. London: Tavistock.

Brannen, J. and Collard, J. (1982) *Marriages in Trouble*. London: Tavistock.

Brenton, M. (1985) *The Voluntary Sector in British Social Services*. London: Longmans.

British Association for Counselling (1984) *Code of Ethics and Practice for Counsellors*. Rugby: BAC.

British Association for Counselling (1991) *Counselling and Psychotherapy Resources Directory*. Rugby: BAC.

British Association for Counselling (1992a) *16th Annual Report 1991/2*. Rugby: BAC.

British Association for Counselling (1992b) *Journal of the British Association of Counselling*, 3(3).

Butler, R. and Wilson, D. (1990) *Managing Voluntary and Non-profit Organizations*. London: Routledge.

Caplan, G. (1961) *An Approach to Community Mental Health*. London: Tavistock.

Clulow, C. (1982) *To Have and to Hold*. Aberdeen University Press.

Clulow, C. and Vincent, C. (1987) *In the Child's Best Interests*. London: Tavistock/Sweet and Maxwell.

Coate, M. (1991) 'Westminster Pastoral Foundation training 20 years on', *CONTACT*, (3).

Cruse Bereavement Care (1987) *Training Handbook for Cruse Branches: Training, Selection and Supervision*. Richmond, Surrey: Cruse

Cruse Bereavement Care (1988) *Confidentiality: Principle and Practice for Cruse Branches*. Richmond, Surrey: Cruse.

Cruse Bereavement Care (1992) *Annual Report 1991/2*. Richmond, Surrey: Cruse.

Currer, C. (1983) 'The mental health of Pathan women in Bradford'. Unpublished PhD thesis, University of Warwick.

Dryden, W., Charles-Edwards, D. and Woolfe, R. (1991) *Handbook of Counselling in Britain*. London: Routedge.

du Boulay, S. (1984) *Cicely Saunders: Founder of the Hospice Movement*. London: Hodder and Stoughton.

Duckworth, M. (1991) 'WPF – personal reminiscences', *CONTACT*, (3).

East, P. (1995) *Counselling in Medical Settings*. Buckingham: Open University Press.

Egan, G. (1986) *The Skilled Helper*. Monterey, CA: Brooks/Cole.

Ellis, A. (1977) *Handbook of Rational-Emotive Therapy*. New York: Springer-Verlag.

Foskett, J. and Jacobs, M. (1991) 'Pastoral counselling', in Dryden, W. *et al.* (eds), *Handbook of Counselling in Britain*. London: Routledge.

Foskett, J. and Lyall, D. (1988) *Helping the Helpers: Supervision and Pastoral Care*. London: SPCK

Gaunt, S. (1985) *The First Interview in Marriage Guidance*. Rugby: NMGC.

Gerard, D. (1983) *Charities in Britain: Conservation or Change?* London: Bedford Square Press.

Glasser, W. (1965) *Reality Therapy*. New York: Harper & Row.

Guardian (1992) Obituary notice: Jafar Kareem, 23 September.

Halmos, P. (1965) *The Faith of the Counsellors*. London: Constable.

Handy, C. (1981) *Working Party on Improving Effectiveness in Voluntary Organizations*. London: Bedford Square Press.

Handy, C. (1988) *Understanding Voluntary Organizations*. Harmondsworth: Penguin.

Hawkins, P. and Shohet, R. (1990) *Supervision in the Helping Professions*. Milton Keynes: Open University Press.

Heisler, J. (1974) *Why Counsellors Resign*. Rugby: NMGC.

Heisler, J. (1977) 'Aspects of the selection process', *Marriage Guidance*, 16(6), Nov./Dec., 414–21.

Heisler, J. (1979) 'Marriage counsellors in medical settings', *Marriage Guidance*, 18(5), 153–62.

Hockey, J. (1990) *Experiences of Death*. Edinburgh: Edinburgh University Press.

Holt, N. (1971) *Counselling in Marriage Problems*. Rugby: NMGC.

Home Office and DHSS (1979) *Marriage Matters: Consultative Document by the Working Party on Marriage Guidance*. London: HMSO.

Hunt, P. (1985) *Clients' Responses to Marriage Counselling*. Rugby: NMGC.

Hunt, P. (1986) 'Supervision', *Marriage Guidance*, 25(1), Spring, 15–22.

Jacobs, M. (1983) *Still Small Voice*. London: SPCK.

Jacobs, M. (1985) *The Presenting Past*. London: Harper & Row.

Kaplan, H. (1979) *Disorders of Sexual Desire*. London: Baillière Tindall.

Keir, N. (1986) *I Can't Face Tomorrow*. Wellingborough: Thorsons.

Lago, C. and Thompson, J. (1991) 'Counselling and race', in Dryden, W. et al. (eds), *Handbook of Counselling in Britain*. London: Routledge.

Leick, N. and Davidsen-Nielsen, M. (1991) *Healing Pain: Attachment, Loss and Grief Therapy*. London: Routledge.

Lewis, J., Clark, D. and Morgan, D. (1992) *Whom God Hath Joined Together: The Work of Marriage Guidance*. London: Routledge.

Lyall, D. (1995) *Counselling in the Pastoral and Spiritual Context*. Buckingham: Open University Press.

Marsh, G. and Barr J. (1975) 'Marriage guidance counselling in group practice', *Journal of the Royal College of General Practitioners*, 25, 73–5.

Maslow, A. (1970) *Motivation and Personality*. New York: Harper & Row.

Masters W. and Johnson V. (1966) *Human Sexual Response*. Boston: Little, Brown & Co.

Mattison, J. and Sinclair, I. (1979) *Mate and Stalemate*. Oxford: Blackwell.

Mayer, J. and Timms, N. (1970) *The Client Speaks*. London: Routledge & Kegan Paul.

Mayne, M. (1987) *A Year Lost and Found*. London: Darton, Longman & Todd.

McLeod, J. (1990a) 'The client's experience of counselling and psychotherapy', in Mearns, D. and Dryden, W. (eds), *Experiences of Counselling in Action*. London: Sage.

McLeod, J. (1990b) 'The practitioner's experience of counselling and psychotherapy', in Mearns, D. and Dryden, W. (eds), *Experiences of Counselling in Action*. London: Sage.

Mearns, D. (1991) 'On being a supervisor', in Dryden, W. and Thorne, B. (eds), *Training and Supervision for Counselling in Action*. London: Sage.

Mearns, D. and Dryden, W. (eds) (1990) *Experiences of Counselling in Action*. London: Sage.

Miller, E. and Rice, A.K. (1967) *Systems of Organisation*. London: Tavistock.

Morris, M. (1955) *Voluntary Organisations and Social Progress*. London: Gollancz.

National Association of Bereavement Services (1992) *Directory of Bereavement Services*. London: NABS.

National Marriage Guidance Council (1975) *Annual Report*.

National Marriage Guidance Council (1982) *Annual Report*.

National Marriage Guidance Council (1986) *Annual Report*.

Nelson-Jones, R. (1982) *The Theory and Practice of Counselling Psychology*. London: Holt, Rinehart & Winston.

Nelson-Jones, R. (1983) *Practical Counselling Skills*. London: Holt, Rinehart & Winston.

Nussbaum, G. (1976) 'Counselling blind', *Marriage Guidance*, 16(1), 19–24.
Oldfield, S. (1983) *The Counselling Relationship*. London: Routledge & Kegan Paul.
Parkes, C. (1986) *Bereavement: Studies of Grief in Adult Life*. Harmondsworth: Penguin.
Perlman, H. (1957) *Social Casework*. Chicago: Chicago University Press.
Perls, F. (1969) *Gestalt Therapy Verbatim*. New York: Bantam Books.
Perry, J. (1993) *Counselling for Women*. Buckingham: Open University Press.
Poulton, G. (1988) *Managing Voluntary Organisations*. Chichester: John Wiley
Proctor, B. (1978) *Counselling Shop*. London: Burnett/Deutsch.
Proctor, B. (1991) 'On being a trainer', in Dryden, W. and Thorne, B. (eds), *Training and Supervision for Counselling*. London: Sage.
Quilliam, S. and Gore-Stephensen, I. (1991) *The Best Counselling Guide*. London: Thorsons.
Raphael, B. (1984) *The Anatomy of Bereavement*. London: Unwin Hyman.
Rapoport, R. (1970) *Mid-Career Development*. London: Tavistock.
Rogers, C. (1942) *Counseling and Psychotherapy*. Cambridge, MA: Houghton Mifflin.
Rogers, C. (1961) *On Becoming a Person*. London: Constable.
Seebohm, F. (1968) *Report of the Committee on Local Authority and Allied Personal Social Services*, Cmnd 7303. London: HMSO.
Segal, J. (1991) 'Counselling people with disabilities', in Dryden, W. *et al.* (eds), *Handbook of Counselling in Britain*. London: Routledge.
Sketchley, J. (1991) 'Counselling and sexual orientation', in Dryden, W. *et al.* (eds), *Handbook of Counselling in Britain*. London: Routledge.
Skinner, B. (1969) *Contingencies of Reinforcement*. New York: Appleton-Century-Crofts.
Smail, D. (1984) *Illusion and Reality*. London: J.M. Dent.
Stanners, C. (1987) 'The levers of change'. Unpublished MPhil thesis, Brunel University.
Stock, J. (1991) 'A study of difficulties in bereavement counselling'. Unpublished Dip. Psy. thesis, Sheffield University.
Sutton, C. (1987) 'The evaluation of counselling: a goal attainment approach', *Counselling*, 60 (May), 14–20.
Thorne, B. (1992) 'Psychotherapy and counselling: the quest for difference', *Counselling*, 3(4).
Timms, N. and Blampied, A. (1980) *Formal Friendship*. London: Catholic Marriage Advisory Council.
Truax, C. and Carkhuff, R. (1967) *Towards Effective Counseling and Psychotherapy*. Chicago: Aldine.
Venables, E. (1971) *Counselling*. London: NMGC.
Victim Support (1991) *Training Guidance: Support for Families of Murder Victims*. London: Victim Support.
Victim Support (1992) *Annual Report*.
Vining, R. (1981) *Training Samaritans*. Slough: Samaritans.
Voluntary Agencies Directory (1992) London: Bedford Square Press.
Wallis, J. (1968) *Marriage Guidance*. London: Routledge & Kegan Paul.

Wallis, J. and Booker, H. (1958) *Marriage Counselling*. London: Routledge & Kegan Paul.

Winnicott, D. (1965) *The Family and Individual Development*. London: Tavistock.

Woodhouse, D. and Pengelly, P. (1991) *Anxiety and the Dynamics of Collaboration*. Aberdeen: Aberdeen University Press.

Wolfenden, J. (1978) *The Future of Voluntary Organisations*. London: Croom Helm.

Worden, J. (1991) *Grief Counselling and Grief Therapy*. London: Tavistock/Routledge.

Wyld, K. (1981) 'Counselling in general practice: a review', *British Journal of Guidance and Counselling*, 9(2), 129–41.

Index

Abortion Law Reform Association, 21
accreditation of counsellors, 4, 39, 55, 84, 117
Albany Trust, 8, 24, 135
Alcohol Concern (Council for Alcoholism), 59, 93, 121, 135
Alcoholics Anonymous, 3
Allen, L., 88
Asian Family Counselling Service, 36–7, 128, 135
Association of Black Counsellors, 38, 128
Association of Crossroads Care Attendant Schemes, 34
Association of Pastoral Care and Counselling, 8, 9
Association of Student Counsellors, 8
Aston University, 10
Atma, R., 37

Balint, M., 12
Barnados, 3, 4, 29
Barr, J., 109
befriending, 7, 20, 27, 33, 43–4, 66, 117, 131
behavioural therapy, 14
Belbin, R., 74
bereavement, 5, 27–9, 32, 34, 40, 45, 49, 59–60, 79, 110, 113, 121
Berne, E., 14
Birmingham University, 10
Black, D., 18
Blackie, S., 51
Blampiad, A., 43
Bolger, T., 123
Booker, H., 7
Bowlby, J., 11–12
Brannen, J., 38, 41, 49
Brenton, M., 95, 99, 134
British Association for Counselling, 8–9, 39, 52, 55, 56, 60, 71, 84, 88, 117, 132, 135
British Association of Cancer United Patients, 39, 59, 135
Brook Advisory Centres, 76
Butler, R., 101, 103

Campaign for Homosexual Equality, 24
campaigning organizations, 21, 24, 132–3
Caplan, G., 118, 131
Carkhuff, R., 12, 79
Catholic Marriage Advisory Council, 7, 23, 32, 43, 71, 119, 135
Cerebral Palsy Helpline, 135

Charity Commissioners, 3, 21
Charity Forum, 94
Charity Organisation Society, *see*
    Family Welfare Association
Child Guidance Clinics, 6, 7
Childline, 39
Children's Society, 29
Citizens' Advice Bureaux, 7, 41,
    57, 72, 110, 112, 133, 136
client-centred counselling, 13, 30,
    87, 119
clients
    allocation to counsellors, 88–9,
        102
    assessment of, 86–7
    help-seeking difficulties, 38–9,
        41–2, 116
    payment by, 65–6
    records, 54, 93
    referral of, 46, 57, 96–7, 106–8,
        120
    terminology, 44–6
    voice, 111–12, 123–5
Clulow, C., 31
Coate, M., 126
Collard, J., 38, 41, 49
Compassionate Friends, 1, 27, 28,
    56, 135
conciliation, 5, 7, 15, 30
Confederation of Scottish
    Counselling Agencies, 71, 120,
    135
Councils of Voluntary Service, 56
counselling
    in clients' homes, 28, 37,
        49–51, 66, 89
    confidentiality, 51–6, 96, 104
    cross cultures, 37, 113, 128
    definitions of, 11–12, 112, 131–2
    early days, 6–9, 15, 18, 22, 65,
        114
    endings, 60, 82, 110, 116
    essential elements, 10–12,
        14–15, 21, 30, 36, 46–7, 51,
        66, 77, 91, 96, 108, 122,
        134
    failure in communication, 35–7

note-taking, 54–5
professional, 10, 84, 117
range of, 2, 4, 5, 19, 23,
    112–13, 115, 131–2
supervision, 12, 33, 51–3, 60–4,
    117–19
telephone and correspondence,
    38–40, 66, 90
terminology difficulties, 43–6
time-limited, 33
training, 12, 13–14, 37, 45, 59,
    66, 69, 81–4, 97, 116, 134
values in, 21–3, 105–6
Counselling at Work (division of
    BAC), 8
Counselling in Education (division
    of BAC), 8
Counselling in Medical Settings
    (division of BAC), 8
counselling organizations
    accommodation, 46–8
    advisory boards, 97–8
    check list, 130
    developing trends, 114
    ethnic groups, 35–8
    Friends of, 48
    funding of, 5, 9, 33, 37, 54, 66,
        99–103, 119, 133–4
    general meetings, 58
    intake procedures, 46, 66, 86–7,
        88–9
    inter-agency collaboration, 95–6,
        107–8
    legal matters, 53–4, 58
    limitations, 132
    local groups, 34–5, 70
    management, 71–4, 91, 92–4,
        97–8, 111–12, 127–8
    national networks, 68–71
    non-counselling roles, 89–91
    off-shoot agencies, 31–3
    public relations, 54, 56, 72,
        100–2, 110
    referral practice, 41, 96–7,
        108–10
    research, 78, 94, 98, 123
    rural areas, 50, 70, 120

safety precautions, 89
student placements, 119
specialist services, 29–31, 121
  see also voluntary organizations
counsellors, accreditation, 4, 55,
    84–6
  collaboration with other
    professions, 95–6, 108–10
  motivation, 24, 28, 94
  recruitment, 74–7
  responsibility of, 12, 45, 91
  selection, 6, 28–9, 69, 76–81,
    83, 119
  spiritual issues, 105
  work contracts, 76
couple counselling, see marriage
  counselling
Cruse Bereavement Care, 4, 12,
    17–18, 24, 28, 34, 52, 72,
    74–5, 85, 90, 121, 124, 136
Currer, C., 36

Data Protection Act (1991), 55
denominational agencies, 105–6
disability issues, 5, 25, 39, 49,
    81–2, 113, 125–6, 132
divorce, 5, 30, 113, 133
Dover Counselling Service, 121–2,
    136
drug agencies, 25, 93, 100, 113,
    122
Dryden, W., 51
du Boulay, S., 31
Duchesne Muscular Dystrophy
    support group, 26, 136
Duckworth, M., 126

Egan, G., 14, 82
Ellis, A., 14
equal opportunities legislation, 54,
    93, 125–8
ethnic minorities, 5, 21, 25, 26,
    36–8, 127–8, 133

Families Need Fathers, 113, 136
family counselling, 15, 113
Family Discussion Bureau, see

Tavistock Institute of Marital
  Studies
Family Planning Association, 7, 41
Family Welfare Association, 3, 7,
    123, 136
Foskett, J., 61, 106
Freedom of Information Act, 24

gay groups, 5, 24, 25, 29, 113,
    114
Gerard, D., 23, 25
Gestalt therapy, 14
Glasser, W., 14
Gore-Stephensen, I., 113
Grail, the, 4, 136
group counselling, 15, 32

Halmos, P., 21, 79–80
Handy, C., 21, 74
Hawkins, P., 63
Haynes, G., 8
Heisler, J., 62, 78, 92, 109
Hockey, J., 49
Holt, N., 4
Home Office, 5, 9, 100, 104, 123
Hospice movement, 31–2, 136
Hunt, P., 47, 49, 62, 64–5, 83,
    123

informal network of caring, 112,
    134
Isis centre, Oxford, 32, 64, 115,
    123, 136

Jacobs, M., 81, 106
Jewish Marriage Council, 105,
    136
Johnson, V., 30
Johnston, J., 122

Kaplan, H., 30
Kareem, J., 128, 133
Keele University, 10
Keir, N., 8, 20

Lago, C., 38
Leicester University, 10

Lewis, J., 6, 7, 22, 98, 105
Lyall, D., 61, 105

Macadam, E., 3
Mace, D., 6
Malleson, N., 8
marriage counselling, 7, 15, 30, 41, 53, 65, 79, 96, 104, 113, 122, 133
Marriage Guidance Council, *see* Relate
Marriage Matters, 5, 123
Marriage Research Centre, *see* One-plus-One
Marsh, G., 109
Maslow, A., 35
Masters, W., 30
Mattison, J., 12
Mayer, J., 35, 50, 123
Mayne, M., 114
McLeod, J., 116, 123
ME (myalgic encephalomyelitis) Association, 114, 136
Mearns, D., 51, 61
media, 57–8
mediation, *see* conciliation
Metanoia, 117
Miller, E., 72–3
MIND, 100
Miscarriage Association, 34, 136
Morris, M., 2, 3

Nafsiyat, 128, 136
National Association of Bereavement Services, 56, 69, 136
National Association of Citizens' Advice Bureaux, *see* Citizens' Advice Bureaux
National Association of Victim Support Services, *see* Victim Support
National Association of Widows, 24, 136
National Association of Young People's Counselling and Advisory Services, *see* Youth Access
National Children's Homes, 29
National Council of Social Service, *see* National Council for Voluntary Organisations
National Council of Voluntary Child Care Organisations, 94, 136
National Council for Voluntary Organisations, 3, 8, 94, 137
National Family Conciliation Council, 30, 137
National Friend, 24
National Marriage Guidance Council, *see* Relate
National Vocational Qualifications, 117
Nelson-Jones, R., 12
non-directive approach, *see* client-centred counselling
Northern Ireland Association of Counselling, 71
Nussbaum, G., 126

Oldfield, S., 32, 64, 115, 123
One-plus-One, 17
Open Door (Feltham), 33, 75, 87, 100, 137
Open University, 118, 129

Pengelly, P., 96–7, 109, 122
Perlman, H., 7
Perls, F., 14
Perry, J., 88
Personal Sexual Marriage and Family (division of BAC), *see* Personal Sexual Relationships and Families
Personal Sexual Relationships and Families (division of BAC), 8, 10,
Poulton, G., 4, 24, 130
Pregnancy Advisory Service, 8, 137
Pre-School Playgroups, 129
Proctor, B., 14, 35, 63

psychodynamic approach, 14, 30, 35

Quilliam, S., 113

Racial Awareness in Counselling Education (BAC subcommittee), 38
racial equality, *see* ethnic minorities
Rape Crisis centre, 29
Raphael, B., 79
Rapoport, R., 59
Rational emotive therapy, 14
Reading University, 10
reality therapy, 14
Relate (National Marriage Guidance Council), 137
  change of name, 17, 21
  clients, 30, 36–7, 107
  early days, 4, 6, 8, 97–8
  management, 92
  payment of counsellors, 117
  principles, 22, 104–5
  relationships with local branches, 70, 73, 119–21
  selection, 30, 75, 78–9
  sex therapy, 30
  supervision, 30, 55, 61, 85–6
  training, 30, 91
Release, 59, 137
research, 88, 98, 122–5
Restart courses, 129
Rice, A.K., 72–3
Rogers, C., 6, 7, 11, 13, 30

Salvation Army, 8, 137
Samaritans, 4, 7–8, 20, 69, 72, 77, 90, 137
SANE (Schizophrenia–a National Emergency), 113, 137
Saunders, C., 31
Scottish Association of Counselling, *see* Confederation of Scottish Counselling Agencies

Scottish Marriage Counselling Service, 121
Seebohm Report (1968), 25
Segal, J., 82
self-help groups, 26–9
Shaftesbury Society, 3, 29
Shohet, R., 63
Sinclair, I., 12
Sketchley, J., 29
Skinner, B., 14
Smail, D., 132
social casework, 7
Society for the Protection of Unborn Children, 21
Society of St Vincent de Paul, 32
Soldiers', Sailors' and Airmen's Families Association, 7
Spastics Society, 4, 8
SPOD (Association to Aid the Sexual and Personal Relationships of People with a Disability), 59, 137
Standing Conference for the Advancement of Counselling, *see* British Association for Counselling
Stanners, C., 17, 18, 28
Stepfamily, 34, 137
Stillbirth and Neo-natal Death Society, 34, 137
Stock, J., 125
suicide, 20, 28, 113
supervision, 12, 33, 44, 51–3, 60–4, 84, 86, 94, 97, 117–19
Support Following Termination after Foetal Abnormality, 32, 137
Sutton, C., 124
Swindon Counselling Service, 66, 137

Tavistock Institute of Marital Studies, 7, 37, 96, 137
telephone contacts, 20, 27, 32, 39–40, 90, 107, 113
Terrence Higgins Trust, 137

Thompson, J., 38
Thorne, B., 131–2
Timms, N., 35, 43, 50, 123
transactional analysis, 14
Truax, C., 12, 79
Turning Point, 4, 138

Venables, E., 6
Victim Support, 15–17, 34, 49, 56, 75, 100, 138
Vincent, C., 31
Vining, R., 77
Voluntary Agencies Directory, 3, 4,
voluntary organizations, 8, 15, 20–2, 25, 52–3, 117, 119–20, 122–5, 128–9, 133–4
voluntary services
  accreditation, 84
  funding issues, 65, 93, 99–103, 119
  as Movements, 22
  partnership with statutory services, 3, 25, 95, 101, 116
  pressures on, 18, 42, 111–13, 116, 132
  publicity, 57–8, 100–2, 103

Volunteer Bureaux, 24, 72
volunteers, 23–5, 62, 66, 70, 76–7, 81, 84–5, 117–18, 128–9

Wallis, J., 7, 65, 85
Wantage Counselling Service, 57, 59, 75, 138
Westminster Pastoral Foundation, 8, 18–19, 59, 61, 69, 105, 119, 126, 138
Wilson, D., 101, 103
Winnicott, D., 68
Wolfenden Committee on the Future of Voluntary Organizations (1978), 3
women's groups, 5, 20
Women's Royal Voluntary Service, 100
Woodhouse, D., 96–7, 109
Worden, W., 59
Wyld, K., 109

Youth Access (formerly NAYPCAS), 9, 138